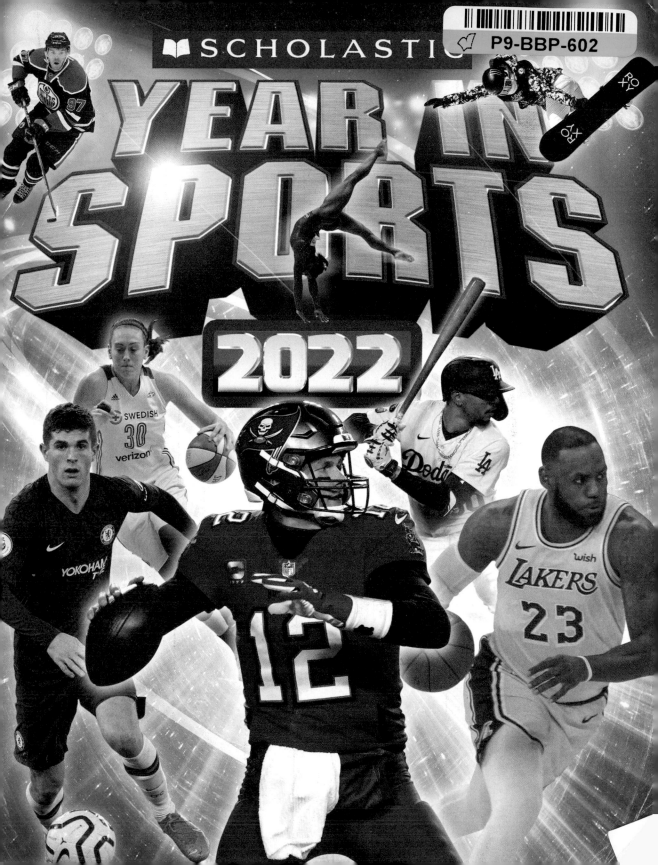

SCHOLASTIC

YEAR IN SPORTS

2022

P9-BBP-602

If you purchased this book without a cover, you should be aware that this book is stolen property. It was reported as "unsold and destroyed" to the publisher, and neither the author nor the publisher has received any payment for this "stripped book."

Copyright © 2021 by Shoreline Publishing Group LLC

All rights reserved. Published by Scholastic Inc., *Publishers since 1920*. SCHOLASTIC and associated logos are trademarks and/or registered trademarks of Scholastic Inc.

No part of this publication may be reproduced, stored in a retrieval system, or transmitted in any form or by any means, electronic, mechanical, photocopying, recording, or otherwise, without written permission of the publisher. For information regarding permission, write to Scholastic Inc., Attention: Permissions Department, 557 Broadway, New York, NY, 10012.

ISBN 978-1-338-77025-4

10 9 8 7 6 5 4 3 2 1   21 22 23 24 25

Printed in the U.S.A.   40
First edition, December 2021

Produced by Shoreline Publishing Group LLC

Due to the publication date, records, results, and statistics are current as of mid-August 2021.

UNAUTHORIZED: This book is not sponsored by or affiliated with the athletes, teams, or anyone involved with them.

Contents

Comebacks!

In sports, writers and reporters like to talk about comebacks. Fans, too, thrill at teams that battle back when trailing to win a big game. People love to see an athlete overcome an injury and return—to come back—to the game she loves. Well, if there was one theme to this past year in sports, it was just that—the whole sports world staged a comeback like never before.

The reason, of course, was the global pandemic. Beginning in early 2020, COVID-19 began spreading around the world. By March, it had hit the sports world and leagues and events were canceled or postponed. Everyone masked up and waited to see what the future held. Now, more than a year later, the sports world is continuing an incredible comeback!

By summer and fall 2020, teams and leagues were slowly starting back up—though mostly without fans in the stands. Players and coaches wore their masks and took their tests. Things were not normal, but they were on the way.

Then the vaccines started in early 2021, and sports were off to the races! There were some bumps on the road back, but by summer, arenas were filling up again with joyous fans, and stadiums were once again welcoming small numbers of people back.

Masks on and knees down in 2020.

Whether in the stands or watching on TV, those fans once again got to see a year of awesome performances across the sports world. Did you see the Los Angeles

The WNBA and other leagues welcomed fans back in most places in 2021.

Dodgers finally win a World Series after more than 30 years? What about when **Tom Brady** won his seventh Super Bowl? He has got to be the GOAT, right? How cool was it when the Seattle Storm "stormed" to the WNBA crown in 2020? And speaking of GOATs, did you watch the Los Angeles Lakers and **LeBron "The King" James** win the NBA? **Naomi Osaka** leaped to the top of the tennis world with two more Grand Slam titles, while **Nelly Korda** leaped to the top of the women's golf world.

The games kept coming back and the fans kept pouring in. By the summer, it was time to watch the Tampa Bay Lightning win another Stanley Cup, and the Milwaukee Bucks climb to the top of the NBA. (There was so much hoops action that we have *two* NBA seasons in this book!) Baseball was back with a full season and some incredible pitching performances.

The biggest comeback of all came in August 2021 when the Summer Olympic Games were finally held in Tokyo. They were a year late, but they were still called the 2020 Games. Fans were not allowed, but that didn't stop billions of people around the world welcoming new golden heroes in dozens of sports.

And now, we're just very glad that YOU have come back to our *Year in Sports*. Here's to a great look back . . . and an even better year ahead!

TOP 10

MOMENTS IN SPORTS
SEPTEMBER 2020–AUGUST 2021

It was the year that almost wasn't. In 2020 and 2021, COVID-19 continued to play a big part in the sports world—to say nothing of the REST of the world! But most sports were able to get back onto the field, into the arena, onto the track, out on the diamond . . . and more. From fall 2020 to late summer 2021, sports fans around the world were psyched to see their heroes in action.

As always, even without fans in the stands sometimes, those athletes delivered thrill after thrill. No matter what your favorite sport is to watch (or to play!), the past 12 months were a reminder of just why we missed sports so much—the joy. It was the joy of seeing the winners win and the underdogs overcome the odds. It was the joy of seeing incredible athletes do amazing things. It was the joy of watching men and women give 110 percent (yes, we know . . . that math doesn't work!) to help themselves, their teammates, their teams, or their countries.

From the kickoff of the 2020 NFL season through the end of the Summer Olympic Games in Tokyo, here's our list of the Top Ten moments and achievements. Yours might be different . . . but that's okay. That's sports!

10

9

8

7

6

5

4

3

2...

10 **ITALY! ARGENTINA!** *Two of the biggest soccer tournaments in the world were moved into the summer of 2021 by COVID-19. Both ended with long-awaited triumphs. At the European championships, England thrilled its fans by reaching the final for the first time. However, Italy had also not been on top for a long time (since 1968), and in the end it was the "Azzurri" who raised the trophy. They beat England in a penalty-kick shootout. At the South American championship, the Copa América, Argentina, delivered a major championship to* **Lionel Messi** *(pictured) for the first time in his amazing career. They beat Brazil 1-0 and then tossed Messi around like confetti!*

9 **HAMILTON BECOMES ALL-TIME F1 RACE WINNER** *By zipping past the checkered flag in Portugal on October 25, 2020, British driver* **Lewis Hamilton** *(44) made history. It was his 92nd Formula 1 race victory, topping the old record of 91 held by German star* **Michael Schumacher**. *Hamilton went on to win the season driver's championship, his seventh, which is also an all-time record.*

8 **NEW GOLDEN CHAMP** *The first events of the Summer Olympics way back in 1896 were held in track and field. They have been a part of every Games since. In all that time, no American has won more medals than American sprinter **Allyson Felix**. With a bronze in the 400 meters and gold in the 4x400-meter relay, her all-time total reached 11. She was 32 years old and a mom in her fifth Olympics, but she ran like a kid. Congrats to our new all-time champ!*

7

SEVEN IN A ROW! *The US women's basketball team has become one of the most dominant in Olympic history. With a 15-point win over Japan, the American team won its 55th Olympic game in a row and its seventh straight gold medal. Two of the players—**Diana Taurasi** (left) and **Sue Bird**—earned their fifth gold medals. That's more than any other hoops player in history, male or female.*

6

EPIC WIN! *The United States has few fiercer rivalries than against Mexico in soccer. So when the two national teams faced off for a Nations League crown in June 2021, fans expected fireworks. They got a lot more than that. Showing the kind of grit that might make them a World Cup team in a few years, the young US team came back twice to win 3-2. A penalty kick in extra time by* **Christian Pulisic** *(pictured) was the winning goal. The biggest play was goalie* **Ethan Horvath**'s *penalty kick save soon after.*

5 **FINALLY . . . THE DODGERS** The shortened 2020 MLB season—most teams played only 60 games—still ended with the World Series. The Los Angeles Dodgers had lost the 2017 and 2018 World Series and lost in the 2019 NLDS. They were due! In 2020, they finally broke through to win their first championship since 1988, beating the Tampa Bay Rays in six games. Dodgers pitching was the big story, with **Clayton Kershaw**, **Walker Buehler**, and **Julio Urías** mowing down Rays batters. **Blake Snell** of Tampa Bay was good, but he was not enough, and the Dodgers danced.

4

THE GOAT

Tom Brady had won six Super Bowl titles with the New England Patriots. In 2020, he proved that it was not the logo that won all those games— it might just have been Brady. He moved before the season to the Tampa Bay Buccaneers and just kept his streak going. Brady directed the Bucs to their second Super Bowl title, and his all-time record seventh. Tampa Bay beat Kansas City 31-9. Tom Terrific took home his fifth Super Bowl MVP trophy as well. Greatest of all time? Yes, indeed.

3 **GOLD IN THE POOL** American swimmers often dominate the Olympics. It was no different in Tokyo in August 2021. First, the incredible **Katie Ledecky** (pictured) continued her Olympic success with golds in the 800- and 1,500-meter swims. She also earned a pair of silver medals. Her 10 career Olympic medals (including seven golds) are the second-most ever by an American woman. Meanwhile, Australia's **Emma McKeon** won four golds, the most ever by a woman at one Games. On the men's side, American **Caeleb Dressel** won five golds, one of the highest totals ever!

2 A SURPRISE GOLD

An American woman gymnast was favored to win the Olympic gymnastics all-around medal. And an American did win. But it was not the athlete people expected. **Suni Lee** leaped and romped and twirled and stuck landings galore to swoop to the gold medal, the sixth ever by an American gymnast.

1

FANS CAME BACK!

The best thing that happened in sports in the past year is that YOU came back! Around the world, slowly but surely, people got their shots. And as that happened, COVID rates fell and sports fans could return. Teams and athletes were thrilled to see the fans back in the seats. Stadiums and arenas rocked once again. Foam fingers waved, and cheerleaders cheered. It's not exactly normal yet, but it was a great first step. Welcome back!

2021 SUMMER OLYMPICS

ACROSS THE FINISH LINE!
American 400-meter hurdle runners **Sydney McLaughlin** (top) and **Dalilah Muhammad** (bottom) put on a great show at the Summer Olympics in Tokyo. In this race, both broke the world record, but McLaughlin won the gold. It was one of the highlights of the Summer Games, an event postponed for a year that finally made it across the line in 2021!

The American team was masked and ready for action during the Opening Ceremonies.

Worth the Wait!

A year late, the 2020 Summer Olympics began on July 30, 2021, in Tokyo, Japan. The Games were postponed for a year by COVID-19, of course. For a long time, many thought the whole event would not even happen. In the end, fans were not allowed at nearly all events, and some athletes and coaches tested positive and were not able to compete. It was not perfect, but everyone seemed to do the best they could.

Another big story before the Games was that the country of Russia was banned for breaking rules about illegal performance-

enhancing drugs. But its athletes were allowed to compete under the Russian Olympic Committee banner. Their national anthem would not be played, but they fought hard for medals just the same.

As always, American teams and athletes were expected to do very well. The World Cup–winning women's soccer team only won a bronze medal and the baseball and softball teams only won silver. However, the women's and men's basketball teams swooped to gold! The women's water polo and volleyball teams were also golden. As you'll see in the following pages, those teams were not alone: US individual athletes also brought home a huge haul of medals.

The biggest news of the first week of the Games came when American gymnast **Simone Biles** pulled herself out of the team competition. She took one vault and didn't feel right. She said she needed to step away for her mental health and safety. Her teammates and most of the sports world offered the world champion a huge amount of support. She was able to return to earn a bronze on the balance beam.

Meanwhile, new gymnastics stars rose, cheered on by Biles. American track stars set records and won medals. And American swimmers were the splashing best. The US won the overall medal race, too (see box).

Of course, the Olympics is much, much more than the Americans. One of the

MEDAL TABLE

COUNTRY	TOTAL	G	S	B
1. **United States**	113	39	41	33
2. **China**	88	38	32	18
3. **ROC***	71	20	28	23
4. **Great Britain**	65	22	21	22
5. **Japan**	58	27	14	17
6. **Australia**	46	17	7	22
7. **Italy**	40	10	10	20
8. **Germany**	37	10	11	16
9. **Netherlands**	36	10	12	14
10. **France**	33	10	12	11

*Russian Olympic Committee

Kevin Durant helped the men win gold.

most fun things about the Tokyo Games was seeing so many countries earn their first—or very rare—medals. And in some of the Games' biggest events, winners came from some very surprising places, based on results from history.

We can't fit all of the Olympics in here, but we did our best on the following pages to find the biggest and most interesting stories. Let the Reading Games begin!

Gymnastics

the event, squeaking past **Rebeca Andrade**, who won silver for Brazil's first-ever gymnastics medal. Lee grew up in Minnesota and her family is originally from a Cambodian people called Hmong. They cheered like crazy back home watching her score a 13.7 on the floor exercise, the final event of the all-around. That put her total score just 0.2 points ahead of Andrade, but enough to make Lee the champion.

Suni Lee leaped to all-around gold!

After **Simone Biles** had to step away, the US women battled to a silver medal in the team event, even without Biles. The Russian Olympic Committee (ROC) team won the gold.

In the all-around, an American gymnast won the gold medal . . . but it was not Simone Biles as expected. Instead of Biles, **Suni Lee** won

Jade Carey was tops in floor exercises.

Winning gold was not new for the United States, though. Lee was the sixth American woman to win gold in the Olympics' most famous event.

An American woman won the floor exercises gold medal . . . but it was not Simone Biles! **Jade Carey** flipped and spun and flew to the championship during the individual event finals. She was added to the event after Biles

Skinner's story was one of the coolest of the Games!

was unable to take part, and took full advantage. Lee won bronze in the uneven parallel bars, while **MyKayla Skinner** earned silver in the vault. Skinner completed a great story: She was an alternate in 2016 when the US won a team gold. And she was not supposed to be in the vault . . . until Biles did not take part. Biles came back to win a balance beam bronze.

MEN'S GYMNASTICS

A team from Russia won the men's competition . . . sort of. The country of Russia was banned from the Games for breaking rules about illegal drugs (see page 20). But Russian gymnasts celebrated winning the gold by only .103 point ahead of Japan. **Nakita Nagornyy**'s floor exercise scored just enough to put them into first place, setting off a Russian celebration.

Japan was home to the all-around champion, however. **Daiki Hashimoto** finished just ahead of China's **Xiao Ruoteng**. It was the second straight Games that a Japanese gymnast won the top individual honor.

In the team event, the ROC team matched its female athletes by winning the gold medal, followed by Japan and China.

The big surprise of the men's individual events was the floor exercises. With a gold, **Artem Dolgopyat** became the first athlete from Israel to win any Olympic gymnastics medal.

Daiki Hashimoto

Swimming

→ The first big headline was "**Katie Ledecky** Loses." But it should have been "**Ariarne Titmus** Wins." The Australian upset the American to win the 400-meter freestyle, Ledecky's first-ever Olympic loss. However, she bounced back to win the women's 1,500-meter swim and then the 800-meter freestyle race. That gave her seven career gold medals and 10 overall.

→ An American woman won the 100-meter breaststroke, but it was not the one everyone expected. **Lilly King** had won the event twice, but this time, 17-year-old teammate **Lydia Jacoby** from Alaska swooped past to scoop up the gold.

→ **Caeleb Dressel** flew through the water to win the 100-meter freestyle race, setting a new Olympic record. It was the start of his busy Olympics. He won the 100-meter butterfly and 50-meter freestyle golds, too. He was the first swimmer ever to win all three in the same Games. He added gold in the 4x100 medley (he was the butterfly leg) and 4x200 freestyle relays (he swam the first laps). The medley relay team set a new world record! For that race, Dressel was joined by **Ryan Murphy**, **Zach Apple**, and **Michael Andrew**. As for what's next— only four other swimmers have won five golds in the same Games. And Dressel is only 21!

Caeleb Dressel shows off his gold-medal-winning butterfly stroke.

Ledecky was charged up after winning the first-ever women's 1,500-meter freestyle gold.

→ Like Dressel, Australian swimmer **Emma McKeon** won a pair of golds on the final day, including the 50-meter freestyle and the medley relay. She won a total of seven medals in 2021, the most in a single Games by any female swimmer . . . ever! (Plus her teammate **Kaylee McKeown**—similar names, different people!—won two backstroke gold medals!)

→ Congrats to **Peggy Oleksiak** of Canada. Her bronze in the medley relay was the seventh Olympic medal of her career, the most ever by an Olympic athlete from Canada.

→ **Ahmed Hafnaoui** made the final of the 400-meter freestyle with the slowest time. But then in the final, he was the fastest! It was a big up for the 18-year-old from Tunisia.

→ Hong Kong is part of China, but puts its own teams into the Games. **Siobhan Haughey** won two silver medals, the first swimming medals in Hong Kong history!

DIVING

As usual, athletes from China ruled the diving medals. They ended up with 10 in all. No other country had more than three. They won at least one medal in every diving event but one. Leading the way was **Shi Tingmao**, who defended her 2016 gold medal in the women's three-meter springboard. In the platform event, **Quan Hongchan** earned three perfect scores of 10 while winning gold. Not bad for a diver who was only 14 years old!

In the three-meter springboard, American **Krysta Palmer** earned a surprise bronze, the first individual women's diving medal by a US athlete in 41 years! But she was not the only American medalist. Both the men's and women's pairs earned silver in mirror-image synchronized diving events.

You'd jump for joy, too, if you won gold like Jamaica in the 4x100 relay.

Track & Field

So many sports . . . so little space! Here are the highlights from nine days of running, jumping, and throwing!

✳ It's not news when Jamaica wins gold in sprints. They've been doing it for years. But it is news when they win ALL the medals! In the women's 100 meters, **Elaine Thompson-Herah** won her second straight gold medal in this superfast event. She was joined by two countrywomen on the medal stand—**Shelly-Ann Fraser-Pryce** and **Shericka Jackson**. Thompson-Herah also became the first woman to win both the 100- and 200-meter races in back-to-back Olympics.

✳ The men's high jump ended with more than one winner. Qatar's **Mutaz Barshim** and Italy's **Gianmarco Tamberi** were tied after the final round of jumps. The referee of the event said they could have a jump-off or they could agree to a tie. The two athletes looked at each other and smiled . . . and then shook hands before celebrating together as co-champions. It was a nice Olympic sportsmanship moment.

* The first track and field gold medal for the US came in the women's discus, thanks to **Valarie Allman**. **Ryan Crouser** won the shot put by setting an Olympic record with his first throw . . . and then another with his last throw!

Crouser put on a record-setting show.

* The first mixed 4x400 relay was held in Tokyo. Teams of two women and two men raced while passing a baton on each lap. Poland was the surprise winner of the event. Since it was the first one, they set an Olympic record, too!

* The ancient Olympics started in Greece thousands of years ago. The long jump was one of the first events. Not until 2021, however, had a Greek athlete won the modern version. On the final jump of the competition, **Miltiadis Tentoglou** leaped 27 feet, 6 inches (8.41 m) to win the gold.

* American **Rai Benjamin** broke the old world record in the 400-meter hurdle race. Unfortunately for Rai, Norway's **Karsten Warholm** *also* broke the record and finished ahead of Benjamin for the gold. In the women's version of the race, the same thing happened, but both runners were American. **Sydney McLaughlin** broke her own world record in winning gold, followed by **Dalilah Muhammad**, also in a time that would have been a new record.

* In the 800 meters, American runner **Athing Mu** did something no US athlete had done in 53 years—win gold in that event!

* **Damien Warner** of Canada won the decathlon, while **Nafi Thiam** of Belgium earned heptathlon gold.

* **Allyson Felix** earned a bronze in the 400 meters and a gold in the 4x400 relay.

Tamberi and Barshim tied for gold.

Basketball

WOMEN

American women are used to winning the gold medal. They've won all of them since 1984 except 1992. But women hoopsters around the world are improving, so this year's US team had a tough fight on its hands. In the playoffs, the American squashed the Australians. In the semifinal against Serbia, the US team won its 54th Olympic game in a row. Tough defense kept Serbia from scoring much, and the US won 79-59. In the gold-medal game, **Brittney Griner** was unstoppable, scoring 30 points as the US beat Japan to win its seventh straight gold medal!

MEN

The NBA is packed with international talent, and a lot of it was on display at the Games. Dallas's **Luka Doncic** put up 48 points in his Olympic debut with Serbia. France shocked the US in the first round, the first loss by an American team since 2004. The US got its act together, and knocked off Spain to reach the semifinals. They faced Australia and trailed by 15 points in the first half. But **Kevin Durant** led a big comeback for the win. It was France again in the final, and the US had learned its lesson from the earlier game. Durant was a star, scoring 29 points in the Americans' gold-medal victory.

The exciting half-court hoops game was an Olympic first.

3x3

The US women held off the ROC to win the first-ever gold medal in 3-on-3 basketball. The fast-paced game looks a lot like playground hoops! **Kelsey Plum** (left) led the way, averaging 6.2 points per game in the whole tournament. The US men's team didn't even qualify to play. Latvia was a surprise winner of the men's gold, defeating the ROC team.

Soccer

Canada's team won a surprise gold.

all three of its early games. The Japanese reached a semifinal game against powerful Spain, however. In the other semi, Mexico and Brazil battled through penalty kicks before Brazil won. In the final, Brazil got a goal in extra time to clinch a 2-1 win to defend its 2016 gold.

WOMEN

The American team expected to romp through this tournament. Not so fast, said Sweden. The Swedes beat the US in the opener 3-0. That snapped a 44-game winning streak for the US and was its worst loss since 2007. The Americans then beat New Zealand and tied Australia, squeaking into the next round. In the quarterfinal, they outlasted a tough Netherlands team in a penalty-kick shootout. In the semifinal, the Americans could not score. They gave up a penalty kick and lost to Canada 1-0. In the gold-medal game, Canada won its first Olympic title, shocking Sweden in penalty kicks. The US beat Australia 4-3 for the bronze medal.

MEN

Some of the sport's biggest countries didn't make the final group of eight in Tokyo. Germany, France, and Argentina were all knocked out in the opening round. Home country Japan looked very strong, winning

Brazil sneaked by Spain to win gold.

On the Diamond

Baseball

Israel is not exactly a world baseball power. They had never qualified a team in the Olympics. But in 2021, their first team did pretty well. They beat South Korea in a knockout game to reach the semifinals. The usually-strong American team did well, but lost a close game to Japan. That put them in a tough spot, but they came through with a 7-2 win over South Korea. In the gold-medal game against Japan, it's probably a good thing no fans were allowed, because the US team would have been deafened! Even without their disappointed fans behind them, Japan beat the Americans 2-0.

Softball

This sport was added back just for these Games at Japan's request. Host countries get to add a few sports, and Japan picked a winner. They beat the US 2-0 in the gold-medal match. The US had won an earlier matchup 2-1, but couldn't find a way to score in the final. It could have been worse; **Janie Reed** reached over the outfield fence to rob Japan of a two-run homer.

A silver medal is great, but not what the US team expected.

Japan's softball team celebrated its gold, even without its fans!

New Sports

Nishaya skated to gold in street.

to act fast when his board broke during part of the competition. But he got a new one and surfed to victory.

SPORT CLIMBING

Scores for this sport combined points from three types of climbing that mixed speed and technique. **Alberto Ginés Lopéz** of Spain won to become the first-ever gold medalist in sport climbing. American **Nathaniel Coleman** earned silver. **Janja Garnbret** of Slovenia won the women's gold.

SKATEBOARDING

It made sense that the newest sport had some of the newest athletes. **Momiji Nishaya** was just 13 when she won gold in street. Silver went to **Rayssa Leal** of Brazil, also 13, while "old" **Funa Nakayama**, 16, won bronze. That gave Japan a street sweep after **Yuto Horigome** won the men's event. The country's skaters kept it up in women's park, when **Sakura Yosozumi** won gold and **Kokona Hiraki** won silver. Hiraki is only 12! Australia broke Japan's streak with a gold by **Keegan Palmer** in men's park.

SURFING

USA! USA! **Carissa Moore** won the first-ever surfing gold medal for women. She's a regular winner on the pro tour, but this medal will hold a special place on her trophy shelf. **Italo Ferreira** was the winner of the men's medal. He had

Moore nailed gold with tricks like this.

Team Sports

FIELD HOCKEY: Though it's not a big deal in America, it's a HUGE deal in other places. In India, field hockey is one of the most popular sports. Until the 1960s, they won just about every gold medal. But they had not earned a medal since 1980. This year, they beat Germany to earn a bronze medal . . . and a celebration back home. Belgium won the men's gold in a penalty shootout with Australia. In the women's event, the Netherlands and Argentina battled with the Dutch team coming out on top.

HANDBALL: Olympic handball is not whacking a ball against a wall, as most Americans might think. Team handball is a fast-paced game that mixes some basketball with some hockey with some gymnastics as teams throw a small ball around a wooden court toward a goal. It's popular in Europe, so almost every team in the playoffs in Tokyo was from that continent. After an action-packed tournament (check out some YouTube highlights!), France won both the men's and women's golds.

The Netherlands team (in orange) passed and shot its way to field hockey gold.

Tackle! But it's not football . . . it's rugby. Fiji (with ball) landed with the gold medal.

RUGBY: Olympic rugby is "sevens," a fast-paced game with and lots of high-speed running (other rugby games have 15 players). The sport is very popular on Pacific islands, so it was no surprise that Fiji won the men's gold over New Zealand. In the women's event, however, it was New Zealand's turn to win, defeating France to win the gold medal.

VOLLEYBALL: On the court, the US men went home early, while the US women advanced to the finals. They beat a tough Serbia team to win the gold medal. On the sand, it was a similar story with a different ending. The American "A-Team"—**April Ross** and **Alix Klineman**—smashed Switzerland in the semifinals. In the gold-medal showdown with a Brazilian team, the Americans romped again, winning two straight games to clinch the first gold for either athlete.

WATER POLO: You think the NFL is tough? In this sport, athletes tread water for about an hour while opponents whack them above and below the surface. The US women, led as usual by many athletes from California, continued to be among the best in the world. They won their third straight Olympic gold with a 14-5 thrashing of Spain.

Klineman shows off her blocking form.

Olympic table tennis is not like ping-pong in the park, as winner Zhengdong Fan shows!

Individual Sports

FENCING: The US has had a bit of success in the past in this action sport, but saw a first in this year's Games when **Lee Kiefer** won the gold for America in the women's foil.

GOLF: Americans took both golds in this sport. **Xander Schauffele** won the men's event, while **Nelly Korda** earned the title for the women.

KAYAKING: **Lisa Carrington** of New Zealand had a very busy day at the Olympic kayak races. She won gold in the 200-meter single sprint. Then she got 90 minutes to rest, then won another gold in the 500-meter double, teaming with **Caitlin Regal**. Not bad work for an afternoon! She added a third later in the four-person kayak.

MARTIAL ARTS: These sports are a big deal in Japan, so the home fans got a lot to read about (we'd say cheer, but the fans were at home). **Naohisa Takato** won the country's first medal of these Games in judo. **Uta Abe** and her brother **Hifumi** then each won gold in their judo divisions. Judo was created in Japan and first became an Olympic sport in Tokyo back in 1964. US fans got to cheer, too, when **Anastasija**

Zolotic won the first American taekwondo medal, gold in featherweight.

SHOOTING: Americans won both golds in the skeet shooting event. It was **Vincent Hancock**'s third in the tricky event, while **Amber English** won her first. **Will Shaner**, just 20 years old, won the first American gold in 10-meter air rifle, setting an Olympic scoring record to boot!

TABLE TENNIS: In 2016, China won all the gold medals in this sport. Not so in 2021! Japan shocked China by winning the mixed doubles gold. China got its share of medals, though. They won both the men's and women's team golds for the fourth straight Games. In the women's and men's singles final, they were guaranteed a gold when all four competitors were from China! **Zhengdong Fan** won the men's, while **Meng Chen** won the women's. China earned six medals overall in this sport, one of the most popular in that country.

TENNIS: Japan's **Naomi Osaka** got the honor of lighting the torch at the Opening Ceremonies. She'll remember

Hidilyn Diaz was the first Filipino to lift gold!

that much longer than her surprise upset in the third round of the tennis tournament. **Novak Djokovic**, the top men's player, was also beaten in an early round. He had already won three Grand Slams in 2021, so he can't be too sad. Germany's **Alexander Zverev** won the men's singles, while **Belinda Bencic** of Switzerland won the women's.

TRIATHLON: **Flora Duffy** won the women's event. It was the first gold medal ever for the island nation of Bermuda.

WEIGHTLIFTING: Hooray for the Philippines! The country has been in almost every Games since 1924, but had never won a gold medal. That streak ended thanks to weightlifter **Hidilyn Diaz**, who won the 55-kg category. Turkmenistan also got its first-ever Olympic medal, a bronze won by lifter **Polina Guryeva**. In the heaviest men's category, **Lasha Talakhadze** of Georgia (the country, not the state) set three world records while winning his second career gold medal. His two lifts totaled more than 1,075 pounds!

Lisa Carrington was queen of kayak!

MLB

CARDBOARD FANS!

The Houston Astros' mascot, Orbit, was the only "thing" cheering at this game. Due to COVID-19, fans were rarely permitted at 2020 MLB games. Many ball clubs swapped in giant photos of fans (the Mets even used pictures of some players' pets!).

The season was shortened, but the baseball action was just as fast and furious. Find out all about the weirdest season in baseball history inside!

A Short, Strange Season

It was the season that almost wasn't! Because of COVID-19, the 2020 Major League Baseball season started late. In March, teams were in spring training in Florida and Arizona, but they were all sent home. Opening Day was postponed. Many people employed at baseball stadiums across America lost their jobs. But lots of MLB players stepped up and donated money to keep paying those employees.

Over the next few months, players tried to stay in shape. Some pitched to their kids or worked out on empty local high school fields.

MLB listened to scientists and government officials. Several plans came and went. Finally, the games began again on July 23.

For once, catchers weren't the only people on the field wearing masks! Umpires and coaches and most of the players wore masks off the field or in the dugouts. Teams took care to follow all the local health rules while traveling. Fans were not allowed into the stadiums, but some seats were filled with cutouts of fans and famous people! While they were on the road, players didn't go out after the games were over. They stayed in their hotels, watching TV like the rest of us. (Some practiced pitching by throwing into mattresses turned up on walls!)

Fans watching the games at home on TV, or online, were thrilled to see their heroes in action. For their part, the players were excited to be back on the field, even if the ballparks were strangely quiet! In spite of all the caution, COVID butted in! Players on several teams tested positive for the virus. Many games were postponed.

Fernando Tatis Jr.

2020 FINAL MLB STANDINGS

NOTE: Not every team completed the 60-game schedule.

AL EAST		AL CENTRAL		AL WEST	
Rays	40–20	Twins	36–24	Athletics	36–24
Yankees	33–27	Indians	35–25	Astros	29–31
Blue Jays	32–28	White Sox	35–25	Mariners	27–33
Orioles	25–35	Royals	26–34	Angels	26–34
Red Sox	24–36	Tigers	23–35	Rangers	22–38

NL EAST		NL CENTRAL		NL WEST	
Braves	35–25	Cubs	34–26	Dodgers	43–17
Marlins	31–29	Cardinals	30–28	Padres	37–23
Phillies	28–32	Reds	31–29	Giants	29–31
Mets	26–34	Brewers	29–31	Rockies	26–34
Nationals	26–34	Pirates	19–41	Diamondbacks	25–35

Doubleheaders were needed to get most of the games in. Each of those games was seven innings long! Teams were scheduled to play 60 games each, but the Cardinals and Tigers were not able to complete all of them.

It was a very different sort of season, but the good news was that fans still got to root for their favorites. Some new stars emerged, including San Diego's **Fernando Tatis Jr.**, Seattle's **Kyle Lewis**, and Tampa's **Randy Arozarena**. Cleveland's **Shane Bieber** won the pitching Triple Crown, leading the Majors in wins, strikeouts, and ERA. The Yankees' **Luke Voit** was the home run champ, continuing a tradition of Bronx Bombers.

The playoffs were made larger than usual, and all those extra games piled on the thrills for fans and players alike. Read all about every series starting on page 42. Finally, one team came out on top as World Series champs in the most memorable season in a long time! Find out who won on page 45!

Tampa's Ji-Man Choi masks up!

Around the Bases 2020

Crochet made a spectacular MLB debut!

Good Start in Relief:

In the first game of the first seven-inning doubleheader in MLB history, Detroit relief pitcher **Tyler Alexander** added another page to history. He struck out the first nine batters he faced. That tied an all-time AL mark for consecutive Ks.

Welcome to the Bigs:

In a September game for the Chicago White Sox, pitcher **Garret Crochet** became the first player since 2010 to make his pro debut in the majors. With no minor leagues to pitch in, Crochet was brought up to the White Sox. And he made quite an impression. In his one inning of work, he threw six pitches that were clocked at more than 100 miles an hour!

One Crazy Play:

The World Series had a pretty wild play to end Game 4 (see page 45), but there was another one-of-a-kind play earlier in the season. In a Cubs vs. Cardinals game in August, the Cubs had men on first and third with no outs. After a grounder to first, the ball was thrown home to catcher **Yadier Molina**. He ran down and tagged **Cesar Hernandez** coming from third. Then he chased **Jose Ramirez** back toward second. Before he could reach him, he threw the ball to second base. Who was covering it? Centerfielder **Dylan Carlson**! The 3-2-8 result (1B to C to CF) was the first in MLB history since records of this sort began in 1961!

Chicago No-Nos:
For the first time ever, both Chicago teams had no-hitters in the same season. Righthanded ace **Lucas Giolito** of the White Sox went first, blanking the Pirates in August. The next month, **Alec Mills** of the Cubs matched him (and surprised fans) by beating the Brewers. While Giolito overpowered the Pirates with 13 Ks, Mills had only five strikeouts and let his defense do most of the work.

Broken Scoreboard:
On September 9, the Atlanta Braves went wild. The team nearly broke the scoreboard by scoring 29 runs, the second-most in an NL game since records started in 1900. **Adam Duvall** led the way with his second three-homer game as part of a nine-RBI night. Five players had three hits, while three players had five or more RBI. Yes, Atlanta won, 29-9 over the Marlins.

HOME RUN HIGHLIGHTS

As usual in baseball, homers made headlines. Here are some of the new longball legends that were made in the *un*usual 2020 season.

➡ For the sixth time in his career, **Mookie Betts** hit three homers in a game as his Dodgers beat the Padres. That tied an all-time MLB career record held by **Johnny Mize** and **Sammy Sosa**.

➡ In August, the Dodgers hit 57 homers, a National League record for most ever in a month. They got seven in just one game!

➡ In a three-game series against the Toronto Blue Jays, the New York Yankees hit 19 homers, a record for a series of that length.

➡ Angels slugger **Albert Pujols** (right) passed Giants legend Willie Mays for fifth place on the all-time homer list. Mays had 660; Pujols reached 662 by the end of the season.

➡ In a game in August, the Cubs became the first team to have all three starting outfielders each hit two homers.

2020 Postseason

AL Wild-Card Round

Astros over Twins:
Houston won two in a row to knock out the Twins. Minnesota set a tough record with its 18th straight playoff loss, the longest streak in major pro sports. **Carlos Correa's** home run was the difference in the Game 2 win.

Athletics over White Sox:
Oakland's great pitching overcame the White Sox slugging, but it took them three games to do it. Oakland won Game 3 6-4 thanks in part to a clutch two-run single by **Chad Pinder**.

Ian Anderson helped Atlanta advance.

Rays over Blue Jays:
The top-seeded Rays swept the Blue Jays. A grand slam by **Hunter Renfroe** backed up a great start by **Tyler Glasnow** in an 8-2 win in Game 2.

Yankees over Indians:
New York won a wild Game 2 10-9 to give them a series sweep. Cleveland blew a four-run lead, rallied, and took a 9-8 lead into the ninth, but then gave up two runs.

NL Wild-Card Round

Dodgers over Brewers:
Los Angeles swamped the Brewers in two straight in an empty Dodger Stadium. Ace pitcher **Clayton Kershaw** led the way in Game 2, striking out 13 in eight shutout innings.

Padres over Cardinals:
Fernando Tatis Jr. and **Will Myers** made baseball history while leading San Diego to a Game 2 win over St. Louis. The power pair each hit two homers. They were the first teammates to do that in postseason game since Yankees greats **Babe Ruth** and **Lou Gehrig** did it in 1932!

Marlins over Cubs:
Miami shocked the Cubs with a two-game sweep in Wrigley Field! **Garrett Cooper** homered off Chicago ace **Yu Darvish**, while the Cubs bats managed only five hits in the 2-0 Game 2 loss. It ran Miami's all-time postseason series record to 7-0!

Brousseau did a happy homer dance!

Braves over Reds:
You can't win if you don't score. The Braves did not allow the Reds to score a single run in their two-game sweep. Game 1 featured the longest run of scoreless innings (12) in postseason history. The teams combined for 37 strikeouts, another all-time record. The Braves smacked two homers to win Game 2 and the series.

ALDS

Rays over Yankees:
After the Yankees set a record with 18 strikeouts in a Game 2 loss, this series was tied. The Rays then won Game 3 and the Yankees stayed alive with a 5-1 win in Game 4 powered by a long ball from MLB home run champ **Luke Voit**. In Game 5, the Rays overcame a great start by Yankees ace **Gerrit Cole** to win 2–1 and capture the series. Tampa Bay's **Mike Brousseau** ended a 10-pitch at bat in the eighth inning with the series-deciding homer, and **Diego Castillo** closed out New York in the ninth.

Astros over Athletics:
The Astros and A's combined to pound 24 homers in the four games of their Division Series. Houston had 13 and those long balls helped the Astros win the clinching Game 4 11–6. Eight players had at least two homers in the series. Houston entered the playoffs with a losing record but headed to its fourth straight ALCS.

NLDS

Braves over Marlins:
Braves pitching dominated in a three-game sweep over the Marlins. Atlanta won the final two games with shutouts. Rookie starting pitcher **Ian Anderson** was awesome in Game 2, while **Kyle Wright** threw six scoreless innings in Game 3. NL RBI leader **Marcell Ozuna** continued his hot hitting. The Braves head to their first NLCS since 2001.

Dodgers over Padres:
The Dodgers had the best record in baseball and they proved it in a sweep of the Padres. **P Walker Buehler** was solid in Game 1. Kershaw gave up three runs in Game 2, but 2019 NL MVP **Cody Bellinger** put on a show. First, he blasted a home run, then he rose above the centerfield wall to rob a homer from **Fernando Tatis Jr.**! In the clinching game, catcher **Will Smith** had five hits. **Justin Turner** also became the Dodgers' all-time leader in postseason hits.

League Championship Series

For the first time since 2004, both League Championship Series went the full seven games. Both series had thrills galore, even if your favorite teams weren't taking part.

American League

The Tampa Bay Rays had the best record in the AL in 2020. The Houston Astros barely made the playoffs with a losing record. But both teams put on a show in the ALCS. The Rays won the first three games of the series. They got top-notch pitching from **Tyler Glasnow** and **Charlie Morton**. Rookie slugger **Randy Arozarena** continued his hot hitting with three homers in the three wins. Then Houston roared back. Thanks in part to a walk-off homer by **Carlos Correa** to win Game 5, the Astros tied the series at 3–3. Morton pitched a gem in Game 7, becoming the first pitcher ever to win four win-or-go-home games. Arozarena hit another homer and was the ALCS MVP. Tampa headed to its first World Series since 2008.

National League

A (**Cody**) **Bellinger** Blast and a perfect relief outing by **Julio Urias** clinched the Dodgers' come-from-behind Game 7 win over the Atlanta Braves. Atlanta had led 3–1 in games before the Dodgers won three in a row to take the pennant. The Dodgers' first win was record-setting. In Game 3, they scored 11 runs in the first inning, an all-time postseason record. They went on to win 15–3 while blasting five homers in the game. One came from shortstop **Cory Seager**, who set NLCS records with five homers and 11 RBI in the series, earning MVP honors. The Dodgers reached the World Series for the third time in four years. They are the first NL team to do that since…the Dodgers, from 1963–66.

Randy Arozarena goes yard again!

2020 World Series

GAME 1 Dodgers 8, Rays 3

The Dodgers broke open a close game with four runs in the fifth. **Clayton Kershaw** bottled up the Rays, allowing just two hits and one run in six innings. **Cody Bellinger's** two-run blast started the scoring for LA; he later robbed a homer with a leaping catch!

GAME 2 Rays 6, Dodgers 4

The Rays evened the series thanks to a great start by **Blake Snell** and a pair of homers from 2B **Brandon Lowe**. Snell was only the second pitcher in World Series history to start a game with four no-hit innings and eight strikeouts.

GAME 3 Dodgers 6, Rays 2

LA starter **Walker Buehler** pitched a gem, striking out 10 in six innings. His catcher, **Austin Barnes**, helped out with a homer and a squeeze-bunt RBI.

GAME 4 Rays 8, Dodgers 7

What a wild finish! Ahead 4-2, the Dodgers lost the lead on a Lowe homer. LA went back on top after on a **Joc Pederson** single. Tampa Bay tied it with a homer from **Kevin Kiermaier**. **Corey Seager** squeaked a single over a diving Rays shortstop to give LA a 7-6 lead. Then came the wild ninth. With two on, **Brett Phillips**, who had not had a hit in a month, came up for Tampa Bay. Of course, he lined a single to center. Kiermaier scored to tie it 7-7. Dodgers CF **Chris Taylor** bobbled the ball, and **Randy Arozarena** tried to score, too. Then he stumbled and *fell* between third and home! But Dodgers catcher **Will Smith** missed the relay throw. As the ball dribbled away from Smith, Arozarena scrambled to the plate and slapped his hand on it with the winning run. Whew!

GAME 5 Dodgers 4, Rays 2

LA ace Kershaw restored order after the crazy Game 4. He threw 5.2 innings and shut down the Rays.

GAME 6 Dodgers 3, Rays 1

Once again, Snell shut down the Dodgers. However, moments after Tampa manager **Kevin Cash** shocked everyone by taking Snell out in the sixth inning, the Dodgers rallied to take the lead. With Barnes on first, **Mookie Betts** doubled. Barnes scored on a wild pitch and then Betts scored on a grounder to give LA the lead. Betts later homered for the final margin. **Julio Urías** got the final seven batters and LA had its first World Series title in 32 years!

Clayton Kershaw

MLB Stat Champs

AL Hitting Leaders

22 HOME RUNS
Luke Voit, Yankees

Marcell Ozuna

60 RBI
Jose Abreu, White Sox

.364 BATTING AVERAGE
D. J. LeMahieu, Yankees

24 STOLEN BASES
Adalberto Mondesi, Royals

NL Hitting Leaders

18 HOME RUNS
56 RBI
Marcell Ozuna, Braves

.351 BATTING AVERAGE
Juan Soto, Nationals

15 STOLEN BASES
Trevor Story, Rockies

AL Pitching Leaders

8 WINS
1.63 EARNED RUN AVERAGE
122 STRIKEOUTS
Shane Bieber, Indians

16 SAVES
Brad Hand, Indians

NL Pitching Leaders

8 WINS
Yu Darvish, Cubs

104 STRIKEOUTS
Jacob deGrom, Mets

1.73 EARNED RUN AVERAGE
Trevor Bauer, Reds

13 SAVES
Josh Hader, Brewers

MLB Award Winners

MOST VALUABLE PLAYER
AL: **Jose Abreu**, WHITE SOX
NL: **Freddie Freeman**, BRAVES

CY YOUNG AWARD
AL: **Shane Bieber**, INDIANS
NL: **Trevor Bauer**, REDS

ROOKIE OF THE YEAR
AL: **Kyle Lewis**, MARINERS
NL: **Devin Williams**, BREWERS

RELIEVER OF THE YEAR
AL: **Liam Hendriks**, ATHLETICS
NL: **Devin Williams**, BREWERS

HANK AARON AWARD
AL: **Jose Abreu**, WHITE SOX
NL: **Freddie Freeman**, BRAVES

ROBERTO CLEMENTE AWARD
Adam Wainwright, CARDINALS

MANAGER OF THE YEAR
AL: **Kevin Cash**, RAYS
NL: **Don Mattingly**, MARLINS

Shane Bieber

Around the Bases 2021

Baseball was (mostly) back to normal as the 2021 season began. Fans were beginning to be allowed into many ballparks. Masks were worn in the dugout, but most teams hoped to be free of them by midsummer. Oh, yes, and the National League got the DH back again. Whew!

Old School Ties:
The students at Harvard-Westlake High School in Los Angeles should have had a day off on April 1. That way they could watch three former students from their school start big-league games on Opening Day. **Max Fried** of Atlanta, **Jack Flaherty** of St. Louis, and **Lucas Giolito** of the White Sox all attended the school at the same time!

Snow Home Run:
Miguel Cabrera has hit a LOT of homers in his great MLB career. But before April 1, he had never hit one while it was snowing in the ballpark . . . and he had never slid into second after he hit it! But he couldn't see the ball leave the yard in the flurries. It was another step on his quest to reach 500 homers for his career.

Mercedes Revs Up:
Talk about a good start: Chicago DH **Yermín Mercedes** set a Major League record by getting hits in his first eight at-bats to start the year. An injury to a starter let the 28-year-old rookie into the lineup. He never gave up the spot and kept hitting. By the end of May he was leading the American League with a .340 average!

Yermín Mercedes

PITCHING POWER

In a year that saw home runs once again on the rise, great pitching performances that highlighted the first half of the season. In a Twins-Padres game, Minnesota's **José Berrios** and San Diego's **Corbin Burnes** became the first pitchers since 1900 to both throw six no-hit innings with at least 11 strikeouts in a game! **Jacob deGrom** of the New York Mets started hot, setting a record with 50 strikeouts in his first four starts (and he was also hitting over .500!). Cleveland's **Shane Bieber**, the 2020 AL Cy Young winner, set a Major League record with a streak (that started in 2020) of 20 games with at least eight strikeouts.

But the biggest pitching news in the season's first two months was the amazing run of no-hitters. There were six before the end of May, the most during that time span in baseball history. Here are the details:

✳ Padres' righty **Joe Musgrove** beat the Texas Rangers 3-0 on April 9. He was one hit batter away from a perfect game.

✳ Five days later, **Carlos Rodon** of the White Sox was also nearly perfect. He beat Cleveland 8-0. Rodon hit a batter in the ninth for the only baserunner allowed.

✳ In beating the Seattle Mariners 6-0 on May 5, Baltimore's **John Means** became the first pitcher to lose a perfect game on a third-strike wild pitch.

✳ Cleveland was the victim again when Cincinnati's **Wade Miley** kept up the no-hit parade on May 7.

✳ Detroit's **Spencer Turnbull** shocked everyone by no-hitting the Mariners. Turnbull was just two seasons away from having lost 19 games in 2019.

✳ Finally, two-time Cy Young winner **Corey Kluber** no-hit the Rangers 2-0. It was the first no-no for the Yankees since 1999.

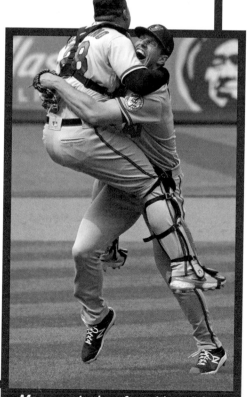

Means got a hug from his catcher!

TOM TERRIFIC!

Tom Brady was already the GOAT with six Super Bowl titles. In 2020, he added another amazing page to his best-ever story. He won his fifth Super Bowl MVP (no one else has more than three) and his seventh Super Bowl (no other player has more than five), leading Tampa Bay to a shocking 31–9 stomping of Kansas City. The Bucs' defense did a lot of the work, shutting down Patrick Mahomes, but Brady was the glue that held the team together.

NFL

Under the Masks!

NFL players are used to wearing masks. They put one on every time they take the field. In 2020, however, masks were seen everywhere—on the sidelines, on the bench, in the locker rooms, in the stands. The reason, of course, was COVID-19. In one of the most challenging seasons ever, NFL players battled each other and the still-active virus. Several games were postponed and some game sites were moved. But the league kept fighting to cross the goal line, and in the end, all 256 regular-season games were played. (A fun trivia note: The 2020 season was the first in NFL history that saw at least one game played on every day of the week, Monday through Sunday!)

Fans were not allowed in most stadiums. Whether they watched in person or on TV, those fans saw a lot of terrific NFL action and some record-setting stars.

It was a season of change for some teams. The biggest news came in March when incredible QB **Tom Brady** moved from New England to Tampa Bay. Without him, the Patriots missed the playoffs for only the second time since

Baker Mayfield

Most games played in front of empty seats.

Herbert charged to a rookie passing record.

2,027

Derrick Henry of Tennessee became just the eighth player in NFL history to top 2,000 rushing yards in a season. He also led the NFL in rushing for the second straight year.

2003. The Bucs welcomed the superstar and headed to their first playoffs in 13 seasons. The Indianapolis Colts also made the playoffs with a new veteran QB. Former Chargers star **Philip Rivers** helped Indy earn a wild-card berth in his first season with the Colts.

Cleveland also ended a long run out of the playoffs. **Baker Mayfield** led the Browns to an 11–5 record and the team's first playoff game in 18 seasons. Buffalo's 13–3 record tied for the best in team history. They earned their first home playoff game since the 1995 season.

San Francisco made the Super Bowl for the 2019 season. In 2020, injuries and poor play sent them to the bottom of the NFC West. The Los Angeles Chargers only won seven games, but seven of the nine losses were by eight points or less. And they showed off the best rookie QB in the league in **Justin Herbert**. His 31 TD passes were the most ever by a rookie.

While some new teams climbed the charts, other teams remained at the top. Defending champion Kansas City had the best record in the AFC. Green Bay, which has won more NFL championships than any other team, had the NFC's best mark. But only one of them ended up in the Super Bowl. Check out page 66 to find out!

2020 Final Regular-Season Standings

AFC EAST	W-L-T	AFC SOUTH	W-L-T	AFC NORTH	W-L-T	AFC WEST	W-L-T
Bills	13-3	Titans	11-5	Steelers	12-4	Chiefs	14-2
Dolphins	10-6	Colts	11-5	Ravens	11-5	Raiders	8-8
Patriots	7-9	Texans	4-12	Browns	11-5	Chargers	7-9
Jets	2-14	Jaguars	1-15	Bengals	4-11-1	Broncos	5-11

NFC EAST	W-L-T	NFC SOUTH	W-L-T	NFC NORTH	W-L-T	NFC WEST	W-L-T
Washington	7-9	Saints	12-4	Packers	13-3	Seahawks	12-4
Giants	6-10	Buccaneers	11-5	Bears	8-8	Rams	10-6
Cowboys	6-10	Panthers	5-11	Vikings	7-9	Cardinals	8-8
Eagles	4-11-1	Falcons	4-12	Lions	5-11	49ers	6-10

1st Quarter

WEEKS 1-4

Seattle stopped Cam Newton at the goal line.

★ The New Guy in Town: Former NFL MVP **Cam Newton** ran for two scores to lead his new team, the Patriots, to a 21-11 win over Miami. Newton also ran for 75 yards, the most by a Pats QB since 1977, signaling that New England might have a very different look in 2020.

★ Nearly Perfect: Seattle QB **Russell Wilson** was 31 for 35 with 4 TDs and 322 yards as the Seahawks outlasted the Falcons 38-25. Atlanta QB **Matt Ryan** was almost as good, with 450 yards and a pair of scores, but his team missed several scoring opportunities in the second half.

WEEK 1

★ Brady the Buc!: The strangest sight of the 2020 NFL season was not the empty stadiums—it was seeing **Tom Brady** in Tampa Bay gear! The six-time Super Bowl champ (with the Patriots) lost his first game with the Bucs. He threw two interceptions, one a pick-six. On the other side, the Saints' **Drew Brees**, the league's *other* famous 40-year-old QB, threw for two touchdowns and New Orleans won 34-23.

★ Comebacks All Over: Six NFL teams won after falling behind in the fourth quarter. The most dramatic was by the Bears, who trailed 23-6 before **Mitchell Trubisky** threw 3 TD passes in the final 14 minutes to win 27-23. In its first game after retiring its old and much-disliked name, the Washington Football Team scored 20 points in the second half to rally for a 27-17 win.

WEEK 2

★ Cowboy Comeback: Dallas beat the odds and **Greg Zuerlein** kicked a game-winning field goal with no time left to complete a shocking 40-39 win over Atlanta. The computers gave the Falcons a 99.9-percent chance of winning when they went up 39-30 with less than three minutes left. But **Dak Prescott** scored his third rushing TD, and the 'Boys recovered the onside kick that led to the winning FG. Atlanta was the first team in NFL history to score at least 39 points with no turnovers . . . and lose! Up to this game, teams with at least 39 points and zero turnovers had 440 wins and zero losses.

★ One Play Short: Newton nearly pulled off a comeback of his own. However, his final-play run was stopped at the goal line by the Seattle defense. The Seahawks hung on to win 35-30. Russell Wilson had 5 TD passes to five different receivers in the game.

✸ Pack Power: Green Bay became the eighth team ever with 40 or more points in its first two games. In a 42-21 win over Detroit, the Packers featured RB **Aaron Jones**, who ran for 168 yards and 2 TDs, while also catching a TD pass.

WEEK 3

✸ Tough Break: The Rams felt like they were robbed in losing 35-32 to the Bills. A questionable penalty on a fourth-down incompletion gave Buffalo another shot. **Josh Allen** then threw his fourth TD pass for the winning points.

✸ Falcons Fade Again: For the second straight week, the Falcons lost after leading late in the game. For the second time in three weeks, the Bears *won* after trailing late in the game! Chicago won 30-26 as QB **Nick Foles** threw 3 TDs and came back from 16 points behind.

✸ It's Good!: Stephen Gostkowski is no stranger to game-winning field goals. He made lots in 14 seasons with the Patriots. For his new team, the Tennessee Titans, he set a career high with 6 FGs. The last one was from 55 yards out and put Tennessee up to stay over Minnesota 31-30.

WEEK 4

✸ Break Up the Browns!: **Odell Beckham Jr.** ran wild against the Cowboys' defense and led his team to an upset 49-38 in Dallas. Beckham caught 2 TD passes from **Baker Mayfield**. After

Prescott led his 'Boys to 24 points in the fourth quarter to close the gap, Beckham ran 50 yards around the right end for the clinching TD.

✸ Saints Alive: New Orleans quickly trailed the Lions 14-0. No problem. Brees led the Saints to 35 unanswered points for what ended as a 35-29 win. Brees threw a pair of scores to **Tre'Quan Smith**. **Latavius Murray** ran for a pair of TDs as well.

✸ Big Bad Bills: Buffalo stayed undefeated at 4-0 with a 30-23 win over the Las Vegas Raiders. Josh Allen again led the way with a pair of TD passes and a rushing TD. Buffalo was the top-scoring team in the AFC after four games.

Buffalo had a new hero at QB.

2nd Quarter
WEEKS 5-9

WEEK 5

✱ Good News, Very Bad News:
Dallas enjoyed a comeback victory over the Giants 37-34, thanks to a long catch by **Michael Gallup** and a game-winning field goal by **Greg Zuerlein**. However, earlier in the game, the Cowboys lost their awesome QB **Dak Prescott** to a scary ankle injury. Prescott was on a big roll, with more than 400 yards passing in three straight games. **Andy Dalton** jumped in to replace him, but it was a big loss for Big D.

✱ Raiders Rock!:
The Chiefs were riding a 13-game winning streak, including a W in last season's Super Bowl, but then the Raiders came to town. QB **Derek Carr** threw 3 TD passes and led Las Vegas to a surprise 40-32 win, handing KC its first loss of the season.

Carr (4) led the way to Oakland's big win.

✱ Wonderful Wilson:
Seattle QB **Russell Wilson** pulled another rabbit out of the hat. The player who has led more fourth-quarter comebacks since entering the league in 2012 added another one over the Vikings 27-26. Wilson steered a 94-yard drive in the final two minutes. He hit **DK Metcalf** on a fourth-and-goal six-yard TD pass with just 15 seconds left. Whew!

WEEK 6

✱ Oh for "Two":
Two teams tried to make two-point plays and both failed—and both lost! After a late TD, Washington tried for two to take a lead against the New York Giants. The pass didn't make it into the end zone, and the Giants won 20-19. Houston chose to go for two against Tennessee instead of kicking an extra point. They didn't score and that let Tennessee tie the game with four seconds left. In OT, the Titans' **Derrick Henry** scored his second TD of the game for a 42-36 win.

✱ Brady vs. Rodgers:
Two of the NFL's all-time great QBs met up when **Tom Brady**'s Bucs battled **Aaron Rodgers**'s Packers. But it was the Tampa Bay D, with two interceptions, that won the day. Brady did hit TE **Rob Gronkowski** for a TD as part of his team's 38-10 win.

WEEK 7

✱ Cardinals Fly in OT:
Arizona completed a big comeback by kicking a game-winning field goal in overtime to beat Seattle 37-34. The Cardinals trailed 34-24

in the fourth quarter, but QB **Kyler Murray** led them to a tie. In overtime, the Cards' D picked off a Seattle pass to set up the game-winning kick.

✱ Big Bad Browns: Trailing by
three with just over a minute left, **Baker Mayfield** and the Browns had the Cincinnati Bengals right where they wanted them. The rising star QB led his team on a quick march that ended with a fantastic 24-yard catch by **Donovan Peoples-Jones** with just 11 seconds left. That gave the Browns a 37-34 win and a surprising 5-2 record.

WEEK 8

✱ Cookin' TDs: Minnesota RB **Dalvin Cook** scored 4 TDs, including three on the ground, to lead his team to a 28-22 upset of the Packers. Green Bay WR **Davante Adams** nearly matched Cook with three scores, but a late fumble recovery by the Vikings sealed the win.

✱ Touchdown Bingo: The Dolphins
checked off all the touchdown boxes on their scorecard in a 28-17 upset of the Rams. The Dolphins scored on a run, a pass, a turnover return (**Andrew Van Ginkel** carried a fumble 78 yards), and a kick return (**Jakeem Grant**'s punt-return TD of 88 yards). Rookie QB **Tua Tagovailoa** got his first start for Miami and his first NFL TD pass. The Rams became the second NFL team ever to give up less than 150 yards and gain more than 450 . . . and lose!

✱ Can't Close the Deal: For a
record fourth consecutive game in 2020, the LA Chargers blew a lead of 17 or more points. No NFL team has ever done that.

Ebron hurdled Dallas for the winning TD.

The Chargers lost three of those games, including Week 8's 31-30 loss to Denver, decided on the game's final play by a **Drew Lock** TD pass . . . and the all-important PAT!

WEEK 9

✱ Still Perfect: Pittsburgh's run as
the only undefeated team continued, but it took a lot of work. The Steelers mostly trailed the Cowboys in Dallas until **Ben Roethlisberger** led a fourth-quarter drive that led to a TD pass to **Eric Ebron** with just over two minutes left. The 24-19 victory made the Steelers 8–0, their best start ever!

✱ Battle of the Old Guys: Drew
Brees (41 and 650) and **Tom Brady** (43 and 651) entered the game with a combined 84 years of age and 1,301 career TD passes. When the game was over, Brees had moved back atop the career TD list after adding four more to his total. The Saints won 38-3.

3rd Quarter
WEEKS 10–13

WEEK 10

✱ Amazing Endings: Two games in Week 10 ended on incredible plays. First, Arizona WR **DeAndre Hopkins** outjumped three Bills defenders in the end zone. He landed with the ball and gave the Cardinals a surprising 32-30 win over Buffalo. In the Lions' game against Washington, kicker **Matt Prater** booted a 59-yard field goal on the final play to give his team a 30-27 win.

✱ Battle for First: In the NFC West, the Seahawks and Rams were battling for first place. They met in Week 10 and LA's defense shut down the exciting **Russell Wilson** and company. The Rams sacked Wilson six times, picked off two of his passes, and recovered a fumble. **Malcolm Brown** scored twice and **Darrell Henderson** also had a rushing TD in the Rams' 23-16 win.

Hopkins's great grab was named NFL Play of the Year!

WEEK 11

✱ Double Overtime: Two games needed extra time in Week 11. A late field goal helped the Packers tie the Colts, but a fumble in OT led to **Rodrigo Blankenship**'s game-winning field goal. The Colts stayed on top of the AFC South with a 34-31 win. The Titans kept pace with the Colts by coming back to beat Baltimore. Star RB **Derrick Henry** broke off a 29-yard TD run in OT for the 30-24 win.

✱ Bad for Bengals: Cincinnati suffered two losses on the same day. In the game, they lost to Washington 20-9. The bigger loss, though, came when rookie star QB **Joe Burrow** suffered a knee injury. He was having a solid season, on the way to possibly breaking the rookie passing yards record. Burrow will not return until 2021.

✱ Revenge:

Kansas City entered Week 11 with just one loss, in Week 5 to the Raiders. They got their revenge in Las Vegas. **Patrick Mahomes** led a fourth-quarter drive that ended with a go-ahead TD pass to TE **Travis Kelce**. Though the Raiders gave the Chiefs another great game, it was KC's turn to win, 35-31.

Kendall Hinton

WEEK 12

✱ Up, Then Down:
After nearly beating the champion Chiefs one week, the Raiders disappeared the following week. QB **Derek Carr** had four turnovers, including throwing a pick-six, and the Raiders were sacked five times. Atlanta blew out Las Vegas 43-6.

✱ Hammerin' Henry:
Tennessee's Henry had one of the best rushing days of the season, pounding for 178 yards and 3 touchdowns. It was his eighth 100-yard rushing game in a row on the road, equaling the second-longest streak since 1970. Henry's running powered Tennessee to a 45-26 win over AFC South rival Indianapolis.

✱ Tough Break for Broncos:
On the Saturday before their game with New Orleans, Denver found out that all four of its QBs had to miss the game due to COVID-19 restrictions. Playing in the NFL is tough; playing without a QB is just about impossible. WR **Kendall Hinton** had played some QB in college, but he had no time to prepare. The Saints swamped the Broncos 31-3. Hinton completed only one pass and threw 2 interceptions. Denver's regular QBs were soon back.

✱ GOAT vs. Future GOAT?:
Mahomes has a long way to go to top **Tom Brady** in the race for Greatest of All Time, but Mahomes's team won the battle in Week 12. Mahomes had 3 TD passes as the Chiefs beat the Buccaneers 27-24. WR **Tyreek Hill** had an incredible day, catching all three of those TDs and totaling 269 receiving yards.

WEEK 13

✱ One Play Short:
The winless New York Jets were just seconds away from beating the Raiders for the Jets' first victory. But then the Jets decided to rush eight players at Carr. That left WR **Henry Ruggs** one-on-one, and Carr hit him with a 46-yard TD with just five seconds left. Vegas won 31-28.

✱ A Giant Win:
Seattle hit a road bump on its way to the playoffs. The New York Giants won their fourth game in a row by upsetting the Seahawks in Seattle 17-12. **Alfred Morris** scored twice for the "Jints," and backup QB **Colt McCoy** had a solid game.

4th Quarter
WEEKS 14–17

WEEK 14

★ Defense for DC: The Washington Football Team scored a pair of defensive touchdowns and beat San Francisco 23-15. It was Washington's fourth straight win and moved it into first place of the NFC East (though they were still only 6–7!). **Chase Young** carried a fumble to the house, and then **Kamren Curl** scored on a pick-six.

★ Derrick Dominates: Titans RB **Derrick Henry** did it again, running for 215 yards and a pair of touchdowns. It was the fourth such game of his career and set a new NFL record for the feat. His rambling ways led Tennessee to a 31-10 win over Jacksonville.

★ New QB = W: **Jalen Hurts** took over at quarterback for the Eagles and showed that he was ready for the big time. He ran for 106 yards and threw a TD pass. Teammate **Miles Sanders** was also a big part of the 24-21 win over the Saints, running for 115 yards, including an 82-yard TD dash.

WEEK 15

★ Jets Finally Soar: The Jets pulled off the biggest NFL upset in 25 years to win their first game of the season. New York came in as 17.5-point underdogs to the Rams, but didn't look like it in the first half. They picked off a **Jared Goff** pass and blocked a punt. It was 20-3 at one point before the Rams rallied to make the final score 23-20 Jets.

★ Dolphins Sink Pats: With no **Tom Brady** this year, the Patriots missed the playoffs for the first time in 12 years. They were knocked out for good in a 22-12 loss to the Dolphins. Rookie QB **Tua Tagovailoa** scored two short runs to lead the way for the Fins.

WEEK 16

★ Six Sixes!: Saints RB **Alvin Kamara** scored 6 rushing touchdowns in his team's 52-33 win over the Vikings. That tied an all-time NFL record set way back in 1929. (Hall of Famer **Ernie Nevers** scored six times on the ground for the old Chicago Cardinals!) The win clinched the NFC South title for New Orleans.

Alvin Kamara

With a hand in his face, Ryan Fitzpatrick completed this pass to set up Miami's big win!

★ Miami Grabs a W:

The last few minutes of the Raiders-Dolphins game were awesome! An 85-yard TD catch by **Nelson Agholor** gave Las Vegas a 22-16 lead with 3:37 left. Miami then went ahead by a point when **Myles Gaskin** caught a short pass from **Ryan Fitzpatrick** and sprinted to the end zone for a 59-yard touchdown. **Derek Carr** drove the Raiders to a go-ahead field goal, but he left 19 seconds on the clock. Fitzpatrick got a chance. As he heaved a pass downfield, he was yanked by the facemask. Somehow the ball got to **Mack Hollins**. With just a second left, **Jason Sanders** nailed a game-winning field goal. Miami 26-25 . . . wow!

★ Clincher:

Pittsburgh won the AFC North title with a great comeback win over Indianapolis. **Ben Roethlisberger** had 3 TD passes in the second half. The 28-24 win snapped a three-game losing streak for the Steelers after an 11–0 start.

WEEK 17

★ Browns Are Back!:

Cleveland clinched its first playoff spot in 18 years with a 24-22 win over Pittsburgh. The Browns stopped a two-point attempt late in the game to hold on for the big win.

★ Titans Bounce In:

Tennessee won the AFC South with a thrilling 41-38 win over Houston. The Titans were far ahead, but the Texans scored 3 straight TDs to grab the lead. **Ryan Tannehill** then ran in for a go-ahead score. Houston tied it with a field goal with 18 seconds left. Tannehill then hit **A.J. Brown** with a 52-yard pass. Kicker **Sam Sloman** bounced his field-goal try off the upright . . . and over for the W.

★ Washington Wins:

After starting 2-7, the Washington Football Team won the NFC East by beating Philadelphia 20-14 in the season's final regular-season game. **Alex Smith** had 2 TD passes.

Wild-Card Weekend

For the first time, the NFL had six playoff games in two days. Here are the results of this football feast!

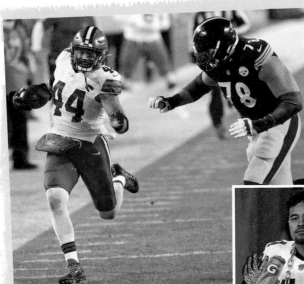

Sione Takitaki had a big pick for Cleveland, then showed off the team's "Turnover Chain."

AFC

Buffalo 27
Indianapolis 24

The Bills won their first playoff game in 25 years. QB **Josh Allen** had a big game, throwing 2 TD passes and running for 54 yards and another score. The Colts charged back late, but their rally wasn't enough.

Baltimore 20
Tennessee 13

Lamar Jackson was bottled up by the Titans' D before breaking out with a 48-yard TD run. The Ravens' defense did a great job to shut down the 2020 NFL rushing leader, **Derrick Henry**. After getting 2,027 yards in the regular season, Henry gained only 40 in this home playoff game. The victory was former NFL MVP Jackson's first playoff win.

Cleveland 48
Pittsburgh 37

The Browns won their first playoff game in 18 years thanks mostly to 28 points in the first quarter. That set a new NFL record for points in the first quarter of any postseason game. The Steelers fell behind on the first play after a bad snap and things never got better. Cleveland picked off four **Ben Roethlisberger** passes, though Big Ben did throw for 4 TDs and 501 yards. **Kareem Hunt** scored on two runs, while **Nick Chubb** scored on a reception. **Baker Mayfield** had 3 TD passes . . . and Cleveland had a party!

NFC

Rams 30, Seattle 20

The Rams had the number-one defense in the league this season and they showed why in this playoff game. LA returned an interception for a touchdown and sacked **Russell Wilson** five times. Meanwhile, injured Rams QB **Jared Goff** came off the bench after **John Wolford** was hurt. Wolford was only in because Goff had recently had surgery on his broken thumb!

New Orleans 21, Chicago 9

The Bears' offense fell apart and the Saints' didn't. After scoring 30 or more points in four of five games, Chicago couldn't get anything going. They didn't convert a third-down play until the fourth quarter. By then **Drew Brees** had led the Saints to 3 TDs, enough for the win. Brees hit **Michael Thomas** and **LaTavius Murray** with passes before **Alvin Kamara** sealed the win with a fourth-quarter touchdown run.

Tampa Bay 31 Washington 23

Tom Brady had won an NFL-record 30 playoff games. Washington's **Taylor Heinicke** was starting his first. But the surprise was that the rookie almost won the game, in part thanks to a dive for a rushing TD. The Bucs needed all of Brady's 381 passing yards to hold off the surprising Washington team.

Aaron Donald led the Rams' sack party in Seattle.

2020 Playoffs

Taron Johnson heads to the end zone!

DIVISIONAL PLAYOFFS
AFC

Chiefs 22, Browns 17

Cleveland made it close, but the Chiefs held on to earn another shot at the AFC title. The Browns nearly scored a touchdown late in the first half, but lost the ball on a fumble. And even after Chiefs star QB **Patrick Mahomes** missed the fourth quarter, the Browns couldn't find enough points.

Bills 17, Ravens 3

A 101-yard interception return by **Taron Johnson** clinched Buffalo's hard-fought victory. The Ravens had come in as the NFL's top rushing team. Buffalo's defense didn't care. They sacked **Lamar Jackson** four times and kept the Ravens' runners out of the end zone. It will be Buffalo's first AFC Championship Game since the 1993 season.

NFC

Packers 32, Rams 18

Too much **Aaron Rodgers**! That's what the Rams faced in this playoff game in Green Bay. Rodgers threw 2 TD passes and ran for a third score. The big play was a 58-yard TD pass to **Allen Lazard** that put the game out of reach in the fourth quarter.

Buccaneers 30, Saints 20

In a battle of the NFL's two oldest QBs, 43-year-old **Tom Brady** outdid 42-year-old **Drew Brees**. The Bucs' D picked off Brees three times, while Brady had 2 TD passes. He also dove in for the final score himself. Brady will lead Tampa Bay in his 14th career conference championship game, by far the most for any NFL player.

CHAMPIONSHIP GAMES
AFC

Chiefs 38
Bills 24

The defending champs trailed 9–0 early in the game, but then showed why they're the defending champs. They scored 3 TDs in the second quarter and allowed Buffalo only six points until late in the fourth quarter. Mahomes was awesome as usual, throwing 3 TD passes. He had lots of help from **Tyreek Hill** (172 receiving yards) and **Travis Kelce** (13 catches for 118 yards and 2 TDs). The Chiefs will try to become the first team to repeat as champs since the 2004 New England Patriots.

NFC

Buccaneers 31
Packers 26

What happens when you add **Tom Brady** to your team? You go to the Super Bowl! Tampa Bay headed to its first NFL title game in 18 years thanks to Brady. The GOAT QB will play in his record 10th Super Bowl after throwing 3 TD passes. The

Bucs' D helped a lot, sacking Rodgers five times. They also created two turnovers that led directly to Tampa Bay points. Brady threw three interceptions in the second half, but Green Bay could only score after one of them and fell short in the end.

Travis Kelce

New team, same result: Brady did what he has done more than any other player—win a ring.

Champa Bay!

BUCS SHOCK CHIEFS AND WIN SUPER BOWL!

Ndamukong Suh led the Bucs' D over KC.

Here's a free football tip: If you want to win the Super Bowl, sign up the greatest player in NFL history. That's what the Tampa Bay Buccaneers did before the 2020 season. Good move! **Tom Brady** led his new team to a 31-9 win over the Kansas City Chiefs in Super Bowl LV.

That was not the result many experts thought would happen. Kansas City was the defending champion. QB **Patrick Mahomes** was one of the most exciting players in the game. His Chiefs had rolled

TOM'S TITLES

Here are all the Super Bowls that Tom Brady has won, more than any other player. The first six were with New England, of course!

7

SEASON	SUPER BOWL
2020	LV
2018	LIII
2016	LI
2014	XLIX
2004	XXXIX
2003	XXXVIII
2001	XXXVI

through the season and the playoffs with ease. Brady and the Bucs, meanwhile, were 7–5 at one point and struggling. However, they had piled up the points lately. (In fact, they became the first NFL team to score 30 or more points in four postseason games in the same season.)

With all the headlines about the offense, it turned out to be the Tampa Bay defense that really won the game. Mahomes was under more pressure than any QB in Super Bowl history! He never had a chance to set up and throw. The Bucs sacked him three times, but put pressure on nearly every throw. They also picked off a pair of passes—both coming on deflections caused by Tampa Bay defenders. The Chiefs managed only 3 field goals by **Harrison Butker**. It was the first time in Mahomes's NFL career that he had lost by more than seven points!

Meanwhile, Brady was busy being Brady. He completed 80 percent of his first-half passes. That was an all-time Super Bowl record for any half. Three of his passes went for touchdowns, including two to former Patriots teammate **Rob Gronkowski**. Brady's calm leadership was a perfect addition to the Bucs' defense and the team's mix of running and passing. While Mahomes scrambled for time, Brady was able to look around and always find the right pass to make. The Chiefs didn't help themselves much with 120 penalty yards, including a Super Bowl–record 95 in the first half.

But while Brady's passing skill put up points, his biggest help to the team came off the field. As soon as he arrived in Tampa, the Bucs believed. His great confidence inspired his teammates. When you watch a guy with six Super Bowls, you learn how to win.

"I'm just blessed to be next to this man," said Tampa running back **Leonard Fournette**, who scored the Bucs' fourth touchdown. "He's the GOAT, the greatest football player to ever play. I can tell my girls that I played with that man."

And we can all say we got to watch him play. Brady was the oldest player on the field at age 43. But he was also clearly the best. Make room for another ring on your fingers, Tom Terrific!

SUPER BOWL FIRST!

Sarah Thomas became the first female official in Super Bowl history. She's a down judge, working along one sideline. Here she is from 2019 without her mask!

2020 Stats Leaders

2,027 RUSHING YARDS

17 RUSHING TDS

Derrick Henry, Tennessee

4,823 PASSING YARDS

Deshaun Watson, Houston

Stefon Diggs

48 TD PASSES

Aaron Rodgers, Green Bay

127 RECEPTIONS

1,535 RECEIVING YARDS

Stefon Diggs, Buffalo

18 TD RECEPTIONS

Davante Adams, Green Bay

144 POINTS

Daniel Carlson, Las Vegas

Younghoe Koo, Atlanta

Jason Sanders, Miami

37 FIELD GOALS

Younghoe Koo, Atlanta

10 INTERCEPTIONS

Xavien Howard, Miami

15.0 SACKS

T.J. Watt, Pittsburgh

164

TOTAL TACKLES

Zach Cunningham, Houston

NFL Awards

COMEBACK PLAYER OF THE YEAR
◀ ALEX SMITH
WASHINGTON

COACH OF THE YEAR
KEVIN STEFANSKI
CLEVELAND

WALTER PAYTON
NFL MAN OF THE YEAR
RUSSELL WILSON ▼
SEATTLE

MOST VALUABLE PLAYER
AARON RODGERS
GREEN BAY

DEFENSIVE PLAYER OF THE YEAR
AARON DONALD
LA RAMS

OFFENSIVE ROOKIE OF THE YEAR
JUSTIN HERBERT
LA CHARGERS

DEFENSIVE ROOKIE OF THE YEAR
CHASE YOUNG
WASHINGTON

COLLEGE FOOTBALL

HAPPY HAPPY JOY JOY!
As the confetti swirled, Alabama's Phidarian Mathis celebrated his team's national championship win over Ohio State 52-24. The title game capped a crazy college football season that almost didn't happen. But it did, and we've got all the highlights and more inside!

College Football 2020

Masks were part of the uniform for everyone.

It was the season that almost wasn't! College football, like the whole world, was thrown for a loop due to COVID-19. Throughout the summer of 2020, fans and players waited and watched. Colleges and the NCAA worked through all the possibilities. Could the games be played? Would fans be allowed? What would be safest for coaches, trainers, and officials? Was it worth playing?

The answers to those questions were different from place to place. Teams in the West had to miss more games than teams in the South. Dozens of smaller schools—and some big ones—chose not to play at all. Games were canceled or postponed at the last minute throughout the country, so teams sometimes scheduled a new opponent just days prior to the game. The Big Ten did not start until late October, and some teams played only five or six games.

The traditional "bowl" season was also affected. Nineteen

Kameron Brown of Coastal Carolina

A Rare Heisman

The Heisman Trophy usually goes to quarterbacks. Some running backs have slipped in to grab a few trophies. But for the first time since 1991—almost 30 years!—a wide receiver took home college football's top trophy. Alabama's **Devonta Smith** caught 20 TD passes, including three in the championship game, to easily win the award.

bowl games were canceled. Others changed locations and most played without fans. The Rose Bowl was not played in Pasadena, California, for the first time since 1942! It moved to Dallas for the January 1, 2021, game.

But let's talk about the games that DID get played! Schools that have been at or near the top stayed there. Alabama, Clemson, Ohio State, and Notre Dame earned spots in the College Football Playoff. All four have been there before several times. However, a few schools that have been national powerhouses had down years in 2020. Texas, Tennessee, and Penn State all turned in very poor records. Their places in the top ranks were filled with schools like Coastal Carolina, Cincinnati, and Iowa State, which all had their best seasons in years. In the final AP Top 25 poll, some of the other unfamiliar schools having great seasons included Liberty, Buffalo, and San Jose State.

Most schools did not play complete seasons, however. All sorts of odd matchups were created. At one point, UCLA's opponent canceled. And then so did California's. So three days before game day, they agreed to play each other! It was like pickup playground football, but in the NCAA!

The playoff games sent two powerful teams to the championship (see page 81). Alabama won it all in a season no one will ever forget. Was it worth it? Seeing the joy of the fans and players after that championship game, you'd probably say yes. And after watching how the hard work of the players, coaches, staff, and more helped so many people during a very tough time . . . well, all we can say is "Thank you."

FINAL 2020 TOP 10

1. **Alabama**
2. **Ohio State**
3. **Clemson**
4. **Texas A&M**
5. **Notre Dame**
6. **Oklahoma**
7. **Georgia**
8. **Cincinnati**
9. **Iowa State**
10. **Northwestern**

September

→ **Great Starts:** Louisiana Lafayette enjoyed the biggest win in school history, when the Ragin' Cajuns upset No. 23 Iowa State 31-14. **Chris Smith** returned a kickoff for a touchdown, and **Eric Garror** did the same on a punt to help his team win. Meanwhile, Texas got off to a huge start in its 59-3 win over Texas–El Paso when **Sam Ehlinger** connected with **Joshua Moore** on a 78-yard TD on the first play! Ehlinger set a career record with 5 first-half TD passes as the No. 14 Longhorns cruised.

Ebner had a busy day for Baylor.

→ **Navy Makes a Splash:** Navy trailed Tulane 24-0 in the second half, but must have called in the Marines—the Midshipmen roared back to win 27-24. **Bijan Nichols** kicked a game-winning field goal on the final play to complete a school-record comeback.

→ **Upset City!:** Underdogs by 28 points and down in the third quarter by 21 points, Kansas State rallied for the biggest upset of the year so far. They beat No. 3 Oklahoma 38-35. A 50-yard field goal by **Blake Lynch** provided the winning points. QB **Skylar Thompson** also ran for 3 TDs.

→ **Upset City II!:** A record-setting day by QB **K. J. Costello** gave Mississippi State a shocking 44-34 win over defending national champ LSU. Costello set an SEC record with 623 passing yards. He had to pass for that many after fumbling twice and tossing two interceptions!

→ **Broken Scoreboard:** Texas and Texas Tech just kept scoring! Texas trailed by 15 late but rallied to tie the score 56-56. A two-point conversion pass by Ehlinger tied it up. In overtime, Ehlinger hit **Joshua Moore** on a 12-yard TD to make the final an incredible 63-56.

→ **Can't Stop That Bear:** **Trestan Ebner** was probably pretty tired after helping Baylor beat Kansas 47-14. He returned a kickoff for 100 yards for a touchdown. Then, after Baylor scored a safety, he carried the free kick back for six points, too!

October

Penix stretched out to score for Indiana.

→ Top Five Showdown: No. 2 Alabama took on No. 3 Georgia in a huge SEC battle. Georgia led at halftime, but then the Crimson Tide rolled in the second half, outscoring the Bulldogs 21-0 en route to a 41-24 victory. They scored 3 TDs in ten minutes, helped by 2 big interceptions of Georgia passes. RB **Najee Harris** led the way with 152 yards rushing and a TD.

→ Down Go the Heels: No. 5 North Carolina was enjoying one of its best seasons when it ran into a Florida State roadblock. The Tar Heels lost their first game to the Seminoles 31-28. FSU's **Jordan Travis** ran for a pair of TDs and threw for another.

→ Big Ten's Back: One of the country's biggest conferences kicked off its season on October 23-24. Indiana put up the first upset when it beat No. 8 Penn State. QB **Michael Penix Jr.** scored two-point conversions at the end of regular time and then again in overtime to clinch a 36-35 win.

→ Almost an Upset: Boston College got a big break when it played Clemson. The Tigers' star QB, **Trevor Lawrence**, was sent to the sidelines as part of the COVID-19 safety rules. BC nearly pulled off a big upset of the No. 1–ranked team. They led by 18 points in the first half, but Clemson rallied behind freshman QB **D.J. Uiagalelei**. RB **Travis Etienne** played a big part, too, scoring 2 TDs in the 34-28 win.

→ Piling on Points: The SEC has been playing football since 1933, but the conference had never seen a game like this one. No. 2 Alabama and Mississippi combined to set SEC records for total points (111) and total yards (1,370). The Crimson Tide came out on top 63-48 on a night when the defenses must have missed the team bus!

→ Gators Get Chomped: No. 4 Florida had its eye on a playoff spot, but took a bit of a stumble in losing to No. 21 Texas A&M 41-38. **Seth Small** hit a short field goal for the game-winning points on the final play. A&M's **Isaiah Spiller** was the powerhouse, running for 174 yards and two key scores.

November

→ **Overtime Thriller:** No. 4 Notre Dame ended No. 1 Clemson's 36-game regular-season winning streak with a 47-40 double overtime win. Notre Dame got a bit lucky when Clemson's star QB, **Trevor Lawrence**, had to miss the game after a positive COVID test. Notre Dame tied the game at 33-33 with less than a minute to go in regulation. After ND scored a second time in OT, they sacked Clemson QB **D.J. Uiagalelei** twice to seal the victory and send the few fans allowed at the game storming the field.

→ **Bad Time-out:** Virginia Tech thought they had clinched a win over Liberty when the Hokies blocked a field-goal try and returned it for a TD. But the officials said that Tech had called time-out just before the ball was snapped. Given another shot, Liberty's **Alex Barbir** smacked a 51-yarder that gave Liberty a 38-35 win.

→ **The Pac Is Back:** The Pac-12 became the last major conference to start in 2020. After two games were postponed, No. 12 Oregon played Stanford. The Cardinal lost their QB and other key players to COVID tests, but Oregon was probably better anyway. They won 35-14.

→ **SEC Showdown:** No. 8 Florida leaped to the top of the SEC East with a big 44-28 win over No. 5 Georgia. The game continued one of college football's fiercest rivalries. It was the Gators' first win over the Bulldogs in four seasons. QB **Kyle Trask** had a big day, with a career-high 474 passing yards and 4 TD passes.

Big Kick!

Vanderbilt's **Sarah Fuller** became the first woman to play for one of the Power 5 conference football teams when she kicked off on November 28. Though Vandy lost 41-0 to Missouri, Fuller's story was international news. She later knocked in a pair of extra points (above) in another Vandy game.

➔ Timely Trojans: For two weeks in a row, USC scored in the final two minutes to win games. First, QB **Kedon Slovis** hit **Drake London** with a TD pass with just over a minute left to complete a comeback 28-27 win over Arizona State. A week later, Trojan RB **Vavae Malepeai** scored on an eight-yard run for the go-ahead TD. That clinched a 34-30 win over Arizona.

➔ Did UNC That?: North Carolina QB **Sam Howell** set school records with 6 TD passes and 550 passing yards in the Tar Heels' game against Wake Forest. He still needed to score a rushing touchdown to put his team up late. Howell had led his team back from being 21 points down before clinching a 59-53 win.

➔ Top Ten Battle: In a rare meeting of Top Ten teams in 2020, No. 3 Ohio State held off No. 9 Indiana 42-35. The Hoosiers were at their highest ranking in 50 years when they faced the Buckeyes, and they came up just short. They were behind by 28 points, but rallied to make it a close finish. Indiana QB **Michael Penix Jr.** had 5 TD passes and 491 passing yards.

➔ New Kid at QB: JT Daniels had traveled a long road to take over as QB at Georgia. He made his first game memorable. Daniels threw 4 TD passes to lead the Bulldogs to a 31-24 win over Mississippi State. Daniels had bounced back from an injury while with USC before being made the third Georgia QB in 2020.

➔ Eight for Six: RB **Jaret Patterson** had a busy Saturday, tying an all-time record with 8 rushing touchdowns. His high scoring and long running (he totaled 409 rushing yards) helped Buffalo beat Kent State 70-41. Patterson also became only the second player ever with back-to-back games over 300 rushing yards.

➔ Down Go the Ducks: The Pac-12's chances for a spot in the playoff pretty much disappeared when Oregon was upset by rival Oregon State 41-38. The final minute was wild. OSU drove to the one-yard line with less than a minute left. Two rushes didn't make it in, and on the second, the QB was injured. Backup **Chance Nolan** had to come in for his first college play ever! With just 33 seconds left and on fourth down, he plunged into the end zone with the winning points.

Jaret Patterson

December

More late magic made USC a winner.

Rice Was Cookin': In one of the season's biggest upsets, Rice beat Marshall 20-0. The Owls were 21-point underdogs, but Rice picked off five Marshall passes. One was returned for a TD. Amazingly, Rice QB **JoVoni Johnson** was the team's backup and had not tried a pass before this game!

Last-Minute Game: No. 18 Coastal Carolina was supposed to play Liberty on December 5, but COVID blocked that game. So they quickly scheduled No. 13 BYU. It was a battle of two undefeated teams, and the quickly arranged game proved to be a thriller. Coastal Carolina's defense tackled **Dax Milne** at

the one-yard line on the game's final play to preserve a 22-17 victory. It would turn out to be BYU's only loss of the season.

Double Trouble: North Carolina runners ran right into the record books in the Tar Heels' 62-26 shocker over No. 10 Miami. **Michael Carter** (308 rushing yards) and **Javonte Williams** (236) set a new mark for combined yards by teammates (do the math!). The pair also combined for 5 touchdowns. In a bonus bit of trivia, QB **Sam Howell** ran for a TD, threw a TD pass . . . and *caught* a pass for a TD!

Timely Trojans: For the third time in five games, USC rallied and won a game in the final two minutes of play. Their 43-38 win was even sweeter because it came against archrival UCLA in a game that the Bruins seemed about to win. A long field goal gave UCLA a lead with 52 seconds left, but **Kedon Slovis** led the Trojans down the field quickly. He threw a short TD pass to **Amon-Ra St. Brown** with 16 seconds remaining for the clinching points.

Florida Shocker: QB **Kyle Trask** and No. 6 Florida had been rolling over its opponents. Trask was piling up record numbers of TD passes and the Gators were 8–1 and looked good heading into an expected SEC title-game showdown with Alabama. Not so fast! LSU stunned Florida 37-34. QB **Max Johnson** made his first start in college and threw 3 TD passes. With 23 seconds left and fog nearly covering the field, **Cade York** made a 57-yard field goal to win.

Conference Championships

December 18–19 were the last big regular-season days for college football. Conference championships narrowed down the field before the College Football Playoff teams were announced. Here are the championship game results.

SEC ALABAMA 52 FLORIDA 46

A pair of powerful offenses kept the scoreboard operator busy. Alabama RB **Najee Harris** led the way with an SEC Championship Game–record 5 TDs. The Tide needed every point they got as the Gators fought back over and over. They had the ball in the final minute but couldn't finish a long drive.

BIG TEN OHIO STATE 22 NORTHWESTERN 10

The Wildcats made a game of it and led for most of the first half. But the Buckeyes had a secret weapon: RB **Trey Sermon**. He rumbled for a Big Ten Championship Game record 331 yards on the ground. That helped OSU control the clock for most of the second half. He had two scores as well, as Ohio State won its fourth straight title.

BIG 12 OKLAHOMA 27 IOWA STATE 21

No. 6 Iowa State had its eye on a chance at the playoff coming into this game, but No. 10 Oklahoma ended that dream. A strong second half and a defensive stand helped the Sooners hold on for the upset win.

AAC CINCINNATI 27 TULSA 24

Tulsa nearly pulled off an upset of its own, but No. 9 Cincinnati ended up undefeated. A last-play field goal was the difference in an exciting, back-and-forth game.

PAC-12 OREGON 31 USC 24

The Trojans could not mount another comeback, so the Ducks won their second conference title in a row. The Oregon defense, led by end **Kayvon Thibodeaux**, was in USC QB **Kedon Slovis**'s face all night long. Backup Oregon QB **Anthony Brown** threw his first 2 TDs of the season to help Oregon win.

Cole Smith's field goal made Cincy a champion.

College Football Playoff

National Semifinals

ROSE BOWL
Alabama 31, Notre Dame 14

The game was not as close as that score shows. The Crimson Tide rolled over the Fighting Irish from the game's first play. WR **Devonta Smith** tied a Rose Bowl record with 3 TD catches. RB **Najee Harris** made everyone's highlight reel when he hurdled over an ND defender during a 53-yard run. Alabama will play in its fifth College Football Championship Game—and there have been only seven in the current format!

SUGAR BOWL
Ohio State 49, Clemson 28

The Buckeyes broke open a close game with 3 second-quarter TDs. QB **Justin Fields** was amazing, throwing 6 TD passes. Two of them were bombs of over 45-plus yards that landed right in the arms of sprinting receivers. And Fields showed his toughness, too. An illegal hit knocked him out of the game for a play—but he came back to perform even better. The win was revenge for Ohio State, which lost to Clemson in this game in the 2019 season.

Justin Fields

Najee Harris plunges in for one of his three scores in the game.

Championship Game

So much about the 2020 college football season was weird and unusual. That made it kind of comforting to see two of the greatest traditional programs ever meet for the national title. Masks may go on and off, but champions stay on top. Both Alabama and Ohio State are in the top four all-time for wins.

Thanks to the Heisman Trophy winner, WR **Devonta Smith**, and a great job by QB **Mac Jones**, Alabama added to that total in this game. The Crimson Tide washed over the Buckeyes 52-24. The championship was the seventh for coach **Nick Saban**. That is a new all-time record for a coach. Saban has won six at Alabama to go with one earlier in his career at LSU.

The game started out hot. Both teams scored early and often. It was 14-14 early in the second quarter when Alabama stepped on the gas. They scored 3 straight TDs to pile up a 35-17 halftime lead. OSU lost its top runner on the game's first play and that really slowed their offense down. Meanwhile, Smith dominated the first half. He set championship game records with 12 catches and 215 receiving yards, including 3 TDs in the first half alone. He later had to leave the game with a finger injury.

Jones picked up his teammate, throwing a total of 5 TD passes. His 464 passing yards were another title-game record. RB **Najee Harris** was also huge, with almost 180 yards from scrimmage and 3 TDs of his own.

WNBA/NBA

BIG BAD BUCKS!
Giannis Antetokounmpo (right) led the Milwaukee Bucks to their first NBA title since 1971. They beat the Phoenix Suns, led by superstar Chris Paul, in six games. It was the end of a busy two years for the NBA, and we've got the last two seasons in this section. The WNBA bounced back into business in 2020, as well; check them out starting on page 98.

NBA 2019-2020
Time-Out!

A masked Giannis Antetokounmpo

The 2019–20 NBA season was unlike any other in the league's history. As another great season was chugging along, the NBA, like the whole world, had to call a big time-out in March due to COVID-19. For months, no one really knew what the future would hold. The league and the players worked with health officials to find a solution.

Before the pandemic stoppage, fans got to watch an amazing debut by Pelicans' rookie **Zion Williamson**. In his first game, he scored 17 straight points in fourth-quarter action against the Spurs. He went on to thrill fans with incredible dunks and physical, all-around play. Warriors fans didn't get to see their favorite player very much. Superstar **Stephen Curry** broke his hand in the fourth game of the season. That put him on the bench along with shooting partner **Klay Thompson** and sent the Warriors into a tailspin.

Fans saw **James Harden** slam through a dunk in a Spurs–Rockets game. Unfortunately, the refs didn't see it and the points didn't count. San Antonio ended up winning in double overtime by those two points—135-133. Another high-scoring game made headlines.

Zion Williamson at the All-Star Game

NBA AWARDS WINNERS

**MOST VALUABLE PLAYER
DEFENSIVE PLAYER OF THE YEAR**
GIANNIS ANTETOKOUNMPO
BUCKS

ROOKIE OF THE YEAR
JA MORANT ▶▶▶
GRIZZLIES

SIXTH MAN
MONTREZL HARRELL
CLIPPERS

MOST IMPROVED PLAYER
BRANDON INGRAM
PELICANS

COACH OF THE YEAR
NICK NURSE
RAPTORS

SPORTSMANSHIP AWARD
VINCE CARTER
HAWKS

Washington set a stack of team records as they piled up 158 points. However, their defense took the night off. Houston poured in 159 points! The Wizards scored the most points ever, in a game a team lost by one point. High scoring was also the theme of an incredible run by Portland's **Damian Lillard**. In six games in January and February, he racked up 293 points. He had 61 points in the first of those games, and 50 and 51 in two others.

In January, the whole sports world—led by the NBA—mourned the sudden death of former Lakers superstar **Kobe Bryant**. He and his daughter, along with seven other people, were killed in a helicopter crash. Players young and old remembered how he had influenced them. The Lakers wore special jerseys in his honor, and the All-Star Game in February featured many tributes.

On March 11, Utah's **Rudy Gobert** became the first major pro athlete to test positive for COVID. It actually happened right before a game. The game was canceled and soon, so was the rest of the season.

After a long wait, the NBA found a solution. The entire league headed to Walt Disney World in Florida. They would enter a COVID-safe "bubble" and play out the season and the playoffs. It was hard on players who missed their families, but it was great for fans at home desperate to watch. In the end, most agreed the results were worth all the hard work. Check out page 90 to find out why Lakers fans were the happiest of all!

NBA in the Bubble

On July 30, 2020, the NBA resumed play. All the players on 22 teams, plus coaches and trainers, lived in Orlando, Florida. They played games without fans watching in person. The first step was to wrap up the regular season and have "play-in" games that would determine the final playoff spots. Here are some of the bubble-lights!

Mr. Bubble: T.J. Warren of the Indiana Pacers was clearly practicing a lot while waiting for the NBA to restart. He scored 53 points in the Pacers' first game back. Then he poured in more than 30 points in three other early games. "He's on a different planet," said his teammate **Victor Oladipo**. A big reason was Warren's accuracy—he was shooting better than 60 percent.

T.J. Warren popped in the bubble.

Surprising Nets: Brooklyn came into the bubble not expecting very much. They were missing **Kevin Durant** and **Kyrie Irving**, their best players. Other players chose not to play in the bubble. No problem! The Nets rallied and pulled off two of the biggest upsets of the NBA's restarted season. They were favored to lose by 19 to the Milwaukee Bucks—and then won! They faced the top-seeded Clippers—and beat them by nine! They were swept in the playoffs by Toronto, but the season was still a win.

Buzzer Beater: In an August game against the Clippers, Phoenix star **Devin Booker** made a play that would be a highlight in or out of a bubble. With the game tied 115-115, Booker got the ball with about seven seconds left. He drove toward the basket on the left, then stopped and jumped backward. As he rose up, he made a stunning fadeaway shot. He landed backward on the floor as the buzzer sounded. Game over!

Here's Booker's buzzer beater.

"Dame" Time: In a game the Trail Blazers had to win to keep their playoff hopes alive, star guard **Damian Lillard** came through big time. He poured in 61 points to lead Portland to a 134-131 win over Dallas. "I didn't come here to waste my time," he said after the game. His most exciting points were his last. A three-point shot hit the back of the rim. It bounced straight up, high over the net. Then it dropped back down for a game-closing bucket.

Mini-Playoff: To add a layer of excitement, the NBA gave the No. 9–seeded teams a chance at the playoffs. In the East, no one qualified. In the West, the Memphis Grizzlies finished close enough to the Trail Blazers to earn a shot in the "play-in" series. Unfortunately for Memphis, they faced the hottest player in the NBA bubble, Portland's Lillard. He scored 31 points in the Blazers' win, which eliminated Memphis.

NBA STAT LEADERS

34.3 POINTS PER GAME
James Harden, Rockets

15.2 REBOUNDS PER GAME
Andre Drummond,
Pistons/Cavaliers

10.2 ASSISTS PER GAME
LeBron James, Lakers

2.1 STEALS PER GAME
Ben Simmons, 76ers

2.9 BLOCKS PER GAME
Hassan Whiteside,
Trail Blazers

299 THREE-POINT SHOTS MADE
James Harden, Rockets

74.2 FIELD-GOAL PERCENTAGE
Mitchell Robinson, Knicks

92.6 FREE-THROW PERCENTAGE
Brad Wanamaker, Celtics

2020 NBA Playoffs

* Facing Denver, Utah's **Donovan Mitchell** scored 57 points, a career high and the third-most ever in a playoff game. Unfortunately, the Jazz lost that game in overtime 135-125. Utah did better in Game 4, when Mitchell had 51 and Denver's **Jamal Murray** had 50. It was the first time opponents each had at least 50 points in a playoff game. Denver ended up winning the series in seven games.

* With a sprained ankle, Dallas star **Luka Dončić** was not even supposed to play Game 4 vs. the Clippers. Good thing he did! After Dallas came back from 21 points down, Dončić buried a 28-foot three-pointer as the clock ticked to zero to win the game.

* Houston's **James Harden** is known for his high scoring. In Game 7 against Oklahoma City, his defense came through. The Thunder's

Donovan Mitchell

Luguentz Dort had a possible game-winning three-pointer lined up when Harden soared high to block the shot in the final seconds. Dort had earlier become the youngest player to score 30 points in a Game 7, but it was not enough.

* Miami's **Jimmy Butler** emerged as a superstar in these playoffs. He got things started by leading his team to a first-round sweep of the Pacers. In the second round, he was the key to the biggest upset of the playoffs. Miami beat the best team in the East, the Bucks, in a shocking five-game series.

* Denver became the first team in NBA history to come from 3–1 down twice in the same year. After rallying to beat the Jazz, they did the same against the favored LA Clippers. Murray led the way with 40 points in the Game 7 clincher. The Clippers continued a record-setting 50-year streak of never making it to the NBA conference finals.

Tyler Herro was a big hero for Miami. He and his teammates continued their hot playoff run.

Conference Finals

Heat 4, Celtics 2

Miami won Game 1 when **Bam Adebayo** blocked a slam-dunk attempt in the final seconds by Boston's **Jayson Tatum**. Down 2–0, Boston got back in the series with a Game 3 win. Four players had at least 20 points. The Celtics were inspired by the return of injured star **Gordon Hayward**. In Game 4, Miami's **Tyler Herro** shocked everyone by scoring 37 points, an all-time rookie record for a conference final game, and the Heat won by three. Miami clinched the conference title when Adebayo scored a career-high 32 points in Game 6.

Lakers 4, Nuggets 1

After the Lakers won Game 1, they shocked Denver in Game 2. **Anthony Davis** nailed a buzzer-beating three-point shot that gave LA a 105-103 win. Denver was in control most of the night, but the "Lake Show" put on a late burst. The Lakers played poorly in Game 3, and Denver took advantage to claw back into the series with a 114-106 win. The Lakers used their one-two scoring punch of **LeBron James** and Davis to win Games 4 and 5 fairly easily. LA earned a trip to the NBA Finals for the first time since 2010. James will play in his tenth NBA Finals, tied for third most of all-time.

Anthony Davis rose above the Heat to help the Lakers rise above the rest of the NBA.

2020 NBA Finals

GAME 1: Lakers 116
Heat 98

Miami sprinted out to a 13-point lead, but the Lakers were just too much. **Anthony Davis** had 34 points as the Lakers romped. They led at one point by 32, outscoring the Heat 77–32 during that stretch. **LeBron James** had 25 points to go along with 13 rebounds.

GAME 2: Lakers 124
Heat 114

The Lakers continued to look very strong by taking a two-game lead. Davis and James each had more than 30 points and looked unstoppable. Miami played without two key players who were lost to injuries: **Goran Dragić** and **Bam Adebayo**.

GAME 3: Heat 115
Lakers 104

The (**Jimmy**) **Butler** did it! Miami's star guard became only the third player ever in the NBA Finals with a 40-point triple-double. Butler had to do it all with two of the Heat's starting players out with injuries. The Lakers looked flat and bored, and Butler took full advantage in one of the most surprising wins in recent NBA Finals history.

GAME 4: Lakers 102
Heat 96

The Lakers moved one step closer to the title with a solid victory over a hardworking Heat team. James led the way with 28 points, but it was a late three-point shot from Davis that sealed the win.

GAME 5: Heat 111
Lakers 108

On a night when the Lakers expected to earn a title, Miami said, "Not so fast!" They kept the game close throughout with solid defense. Three-point star **Duncan Robinson** had 26 points after not shooting well earlier in the

Butler played well, but it was not enough.

series. Butler continued his amazing play with 35 points, 12 rebounds, 11 assists, and 5 steals. LA's **Danny Green** had a chance to tie it with a last-second three-pointer, but his shot fell short. LA would have to wait and try again in Game 6.

GAME 6: Lakers 106
Heat 93

This one was over early, and the Lakers cruised to the title in the longest NBA season ever. LA roared out of the gate, playing crushing defense. By halftime, they were up by 28 points, the second-largest lead ever at the break in a Finals game. In the second half, the Lakers led by as many as 36. James registered a triple-double and was named the Finals MVP for the fourth time in his career. It was also the third different team James had led to an NBA title.

17

That's the number of NBA titles for the Lakers, which ties them with the Boston Celtics for the most in league history. Trivia time: The first five championships for the Lakers came when the team was based in Minneapolis! They moved to LA in 1960.

NBA 2020-21

The theme for the 2020–21 NBA season was stars, stars, and more stars. On both coasts, teams added players that created "SuperTeams." In the West, the Lakers continued with **LeBron James** and Anthony Davis. The Clippers added **Paul George** to a lineup that featured **Kawhi Leonard**. In the East, the Nets were already loaded with **Kevin Durant** and **Kyrie Irving** but then added mega-scorer **James Harden**,

Washington's Bradley Beal

slam-dunk star **Blake Griffin**, and rebounding king **DeAndre Jordan**. Harden paid off quickly, pouring in 49 points in his first game for Brooklyn.

But when the regular season—shortened from the usual 82 to 72 games—ended, some surprising teams were at the top. In the West, the Jazz had the best record. **Donovan Mitchell** was the team's sole superstar, but they played great defense and won 52 games.

Just behind were the Phoenix Suns and Denver Nuggets. The SuperTeams trailed, as injuries kept many of the big names out of games.

In the East, the Philadelphia 76ers reigned, surprising many experts who thought the team was not deep enough. The mighty Nets were right behind, but faced injury issues for the playoffs. A big surprise was the play of the New York Knicks, who had their best season since 2013 and thrilled their loyal fans in Madison Square Garden. **Julius Randle** led the way.

After the excitement of the regular season, the NBA

Harden, Durant, and Jordan were among the stars recruited by the Nets.

presented the "play-in" games. These mini-playoffs began during the COVID bubble in 2020. The league decided to keep the drama in the mix. The last four ranked teams played off to decide which two from each conference would make the playoffs. The Lakers had to battle past **Steph Curry** and the Warriors, while the Celtics had to get past scoring machine **Bradley Beal** and the Wizards. The Wizards were one of the Cinderella teams of the season. They were 3–12 at one point and had to stop playing for two weeks to deal with the pandemic. But Beal led the way to a great rally to earn a spot in the play-in, which they won to earn a No. 8 seed.

As usual, the playoffs saw all sorts of surprises and some dominating performances. In the end, all the big stars except one were on the sidelines, as a young man from far away stood tall as the leader of the championship team. Catch up to all the action on page 96.

NBA Award Winners

MOST VALUABLE PLAYER
Nikola **JOKIĆ**, NUGGETS

DEFENSIVE PLAYER OF THE YEAR
Rudy **GOBERT**, JAZZ

ROOKIE OF THE YEAR
LaMelo **BALL**, HORNETS

SIXTH MAN
Jordan **CLARKSON**, JAZZ

MOST IMPROVED PLAYER
Julius **RANDLE**, KNICKS

COACH OF THE YEAR
Tom **THIBODEAU**, KNICKS

SPORTSMANSHIP AWARD
Jrue **HOLIDAY**, BUCKS

In the Paint 2021

A Real Rebound: In December, the Clippers rallied to knock off the rival Lakers. But just six nights later, the Clips lost to the Mavericks by an incredible 51 points. They were down by 50 at halftime, the first time that had ever happened in the NBA since the shot clock was added in 1953.

Three-Point Record: While whomping the Heat 144-97 on December 30, the Milwaukee Bucks set a new NBA

The masked man poured in points!

record by making 29 three-point shots. They took 51 of them, also among the most ever in a game. **Sam Merrill** made the 28th, breaking the old record, before the team ended at 29.

NBA First: On the last day of the year in 2020, the NBA saw a big first. San Antonio coach **Gregg Popovich** was ejected after arguing with the referees. Assistant coach **Becky Hammon** stepped in to coach the team, becoming the first woman to act as head coach of an NBA team. They lost the game, but it was a big win for women in sports.

Points Parade: **Stephen Curry** has set a lot of scoring records in his great NBA career, pouring in three-pointers like no one before him. But in a January 2021

Hammon stepped into an NBA first.

NBA Stat Leaders

(all are per game except for three-pointers and percentages)

32.0 Points
Stephen Curry, Warriors

14.3 Rebounds
Clint Capela, Hawks

11.7 Assists
Russell Westbrook, Wizards

2.1 Steals
Jimmy Butler, Heat

3.4 Blocks
Myles Turner, Pacers

337 Three-Point Shots Made
Stephen Curry, Warriors

76.3 Field-Goal Pct.
DeAndre Jordan, Nets

93.4 Free-Throw Pct.
Chris Paul, Suns

for the 76ers in a February 2021 game. His team beat the Denver Nuggets. But **Jamal Murray** of Denver also went for 50 and his was special: He tied an NBA record by reaching that total on 84 percent shooting. He was also the first ever to score 50 without making a free throw!

Mr. Triple-Double: With his 36th triple-double of the 2020–21 season, Washington's Westbrook set a new all-time NBA career record with 182 games with double digits in points, rebounds, and assists. He broke a record set way back in 1974 by the great **Oscar Robertson**.

Russell Westbrook

game, he set a personal mark. His 62 points in the Warriors' win over the Trail Blazers were the most he had ever scored in a game.

Busy Scoreboard: Speaking of scoring, the Nets and Wizards lit up the scoreboard in their game in their January 2021 game. Four players topped 30 points, including game leader **Russell Westbrook** for Washington, as the Wizards nipped the Nets 149-146. Westbrook and **Bradley Beal** both hit late treys to pull their team ahead.

50-50: It's a big deal with a player hits 50 points in a game. **Joel Embiid** did it

2021 NBA Playoffs

→ The L.A. Clippers upset the No. 1 seeded Utah Jazz in the second round. They lost the first two games, but then won four straight to send the Jazz home.

→ Phoenix continued its great season, led by veteran **Chris Paul** and emerging star **Devin Booker**. They beat the Lakers in the first round, as LA was without **Anthony Davis** for most of the series.

Young was a huge star for the Hawks.

The Suns then swept Denver and MVP **Nikola Jokić** in the second round.

→ In the East, the Hawks were the biggest surprise. Seeded fifth, they beat the Knicks, to the disappointment of New York fans. Then they surprised the No. 1 ranked 76ers. **Trae Young** of Atlanta pumped in 41 points in a thrilling Game 7 to send the Hawks to the conference finals.

→ They faced Milwaukee there, who had beaten the SuperTeam Nets. Brooklyn lost **Harden**, **Irving** and **Durant** could not do it alone.

→ In the Western Conference finals, the Suns won the first two games, including Game 2 on a buzzer-beating tap-in by **Deandre Ayton**. The Clippers won Games 3 and 5 thanks to big scoring from **Paul George**. Phoenix star Chris Paul then poured in 41 points in Game 6. The veteran guard will play in his first NBA Finals.

→ In the East, Atlanta surprised Milwaukee and star **Giannis Antetokounmpo** in Game 1, but the Bucks roared back with a 35-point win in Game 2 before also winning Game 3. Milwaukee played without Antetokounmpo for the final two games, but still won the series.

NBA Finals

GAME 1
Suns 118, Bucks 105

Veteran guard Chris Paul waited 16 years for this game. It was his first-ever NBA Finals appearance, and he made it a big one. Paul poured in 16 of his 32 points in the third quarter to give the Suns a lead they would not give up. **Deandre Ayton** had 22 points for the Suns.

GAME 2
Suns 118, Bucks 108

In Game 1, it was the veteran. In Game 2, it was the rising star. **Devin Booker** poured in 31 points as the Suns beat the Bucks by an almost identical score to Game 1. Three-pointers were key, as Booker nailed seven of them. Milwaukee got 42 from **Giannis Antetokounmpo**, but it was not enough.

Giannis was named Finals MVP.

GAME 3
Bucks 120, Suns 100

Antetokounmpo poured in 41 points and had 13 rebounds as the Bucks swamped the Suns. It was the first NBA Finals game in Milwaukee since 1974. Antetokounmpo also became only the second player with back-to-back 40-point, 10-rebound NBA Finals games.

GAME 4
Bucks 109, Suns 103

Khris Middleton put up 40 points and Antetokounmpo made a key late-game block of a dunk attempt. The dunk by Ayton would have tied the game with less than two minutes. But the big Greek star smacked the ball away and Milwaukee held on.

GAME 5
Bucks 123, Suns 119

Milwaukee's **Jrue Holiday** made a game-saving steal to clinch the Bucks' third win. Booker was driving for what would have been a go-ahead basket. Defensive whiz Holiday snatched the ball away, then lobbed it to Antetokounmpo for a game-clinching dunk. Earlier, the Bucks rallied from 16 points behind in the second quarter.

GAME 6
Bucks 105, Suns 98

In one of the most impressive NBA Finals games ever, Antetokonumpo scored 50 points in leading his team to its first title since 1971. Only one other player (**Bob Pettit** in 1958) had scored 50 in a game in which his team won the championship.

2020 WNBA

Welcome to Florida! That's what the WNBA said in July when the teams and coaches gathered inside a bubble to play the shortened 22-game 2020 season.

The chances for a great year for the Las Vegas Aces looked slim. Star center **Liz Cambage** could not play due to COVID-19, while ace guard **Kelsey Plum** was injured. Fortunately, the Aces still had MVP candidate **A'ja Wilson**. She worked with the best bench in the league (they averaged a WNBA-record 35 points per game)

Candace Parker had a star season, winning Defensive Player of the Year and All-WNBA honors.

2020 WNBA Standings

Las Vegas Aces	18–4
Seattle Storm	18–4
Los Angeles Sparks	15–7
Minnesota Lynx	14–8
Phoenix Mercury	13–9
Chicago Sky	12–10
Connecticut Sun	10–12
Washington Mystics	9–13
Dallas Wings	8–14
Atlanta Dream	7–15
Indiana Fever	6–16
New York Liberty	2–20

The LA Sparks got another awesome season from **Candace Parker** and earned the third seed. The Minnesota Lynx returned to their usual greatness with 14 wins and the fourth seed. The Phoenix Mercury probably had the hardest road to the playoffs. Due to injuries and illnesses, they had as few as seven players on their roster. And star center **Brittney Griner** had to miss three weeks of the season. Still, they had a winning record thanks to all-time star **Diana Taurasi** and rising legend **Skylar Diggins-Smith**.

Shout out to **Courtney Vandersloot** of the Chicago Sky. She not only led her team to the playoffs, she set a WNBA record with 18 assists in a win over the Indiana Fever. Bonus Vandersloot fun: Several of those assists went to her teammate and wife **Allie Quigley**!

to finish tied for the league's best record at 18–4. The Seattle Storm, meanwhile, were expected to be great…and they were. They were the top-rated team on both offense and defense, led by superstars **Breanna Stewart**—who had to miss the whole 2019 season—and **Sue Bird**. They also finished 18–4.

WNBA AWARDS WINNERS

MVP: **A'Ja Wilson**, Aces ▶▶▶
ROOKIE OF THE YEAR: **Crystal Dangerfield**, Lynx
DEFENSIVE PLAYER OF THE YEAR: **Candace Parker**, Sparks
SIXTH WOMAN OF THE YEAR: **Dearica Hamby**, Aces
MOST IMPROVED PLAYER: **Betnijah Laney**, Dream
COACH OF THE YEAR: **Cheryl Reeve**, Lynx

2020 WNBA Playoffs

The top two seeds, Las Vegas and Seattle, got to sit and watch the first two rounds of single-elimination games that sent two teams to face No. 3 Los Angeles and No. 4 Minnesota. The winners there went to the semifinals.

Round One:

* **Shey Peddy** buried a game-winning, buzzer-beating, three-point shot that made her Phoenix Mercury winners. After the Washington Mystics took a very late lead, Peddy got a pass and let fly to clinch the 85-84 win.

* **Alyssa Thomas** led the way with 26 points and 13 rebounds as the Connecticut Sun routed the Chicago Sky 94-81. **DeWanna Bonner** had 23 points for the winners, who outrebounded the Sky 40 to 21.

Round Two:

* The Sun shocked the favored LA Sparks. A 22-8 lead after the first quarter led to a surprising 73-59 win.

* The Minnesota Lynx send the Mercury home by holding on for an 80-79 win. A possible game-winning shot by the Mercury bounced off the rim.

Conference Semifinals:

Aces 3, Sun 2

Connecticut nearly continued its upset streak, but Vegas had an ace up its sleeve. In the fourth quarter of Game 5, **A'ja Wilson** picked up her team and carried it to the WNBA Finals. She scored 11 of her game-high 23 points in the fourth quarter. Wilson and the Aces won 66-63.

Storm 3, Lynx 0

Breanna Stewart and **Sue Bird** were on a mission. Both missed most of 2019 with injuries. They would not let anything stop them from a shot at another title. They led the way as Seattle swept Minnesota. In the clinching Game 3, a 92-71 win, Stewart poured in 31 points, her most ever in the playoffs.

Make a shot, get a hug: Teammates surround Peddy.

2020 WNBA Finals

GAME 1 **Seattle** 93
Las Vegas 80

We all learned the lesson in kindergarten: Sharing is caring. Seattle guard **Sue Bird** learned that lesson really well! She set a single-game record with 16 assists to help her team jump out to the lead in the Finals. A lot of those passes went to **Breanna Stewart**, who scored 37 points, the second-most ever in a Finals game.

GAME 2 **Seattle** 104
Las Vegas 91

More sharing! The Storm set a WNBA Finals record with 33 assists, with Bird getting 10 of those. Stewart led the way with 22 points, one of three Storm shooters to score more than 20 on the night.

GAME 3 **Seattle** 92
Las Vegas 59

The Storm won its second WNBA championship in three years in record-setting fashion. Their sweep of the Aces made it 11 Finals victories in a row. That's the most in WNBA or NBA history! Stewart continued her hot play and averaged 28.3 points per game to earn her second WNBA Finals MVP award! Bird became the first WNBA player to win a championship in three different decades.

Finals MVP Breanna Stewart

COLLEGE BASKETBALL

DAKTRONICS

00.6

JAQUEZ JR.
4

TIMME
2

ONE SHINING MOMENT

Gonzaga's Jalen Suggs banked in this 40-foot shot to beat UCLA in overtime. The shocking bucket sent the Zags to the national championship with a chance to finish undefeated. Baylor had other ideas about that, as a wild-and-crazy NCAA basketball season ended with a big surprise. To read all about this one-of-a-kind season, turn the page!

One Strange Season

There was one word that dominated college basketball in 2020–21. And it wasn't rebound, dribble, or bucket. It was COVID! The virus caused a delay in starting the season. When games began, they were played, for the most part, in front of empty seats. Players were tested often and did their best to stay safe and healthy. But nobody is perfect, and dozens of games were canceled or postponed due to positive cases.

Pac-12 champ Stanford shows off its masks.

On the women's side, Duke, Virginia, and the entire Ivy League canceled their seasons. Some men's teams threw in the towel, too, including Chicago State and Howard.

But the games went on as often as they could, and some great stories came out of the season. The women's rankings included four different No. 1s as the season went on: Stanford, Louisville, Connecticut, and South Carolina. UConn freshman **Paige Bueckers** made history by becoming the first freshman to be named the AP Player of the Year in her sport. Stanford tried to keep its top ranking even while having to play nearly all its games on the road. The Cardinal also were shocked by the

Paige Bueckers

biggest upset of a No. 1–ranked team when unranked Colorado beat them 77-72.

On the men's side, you might think that taking three weeks off in the middle of a season would help a team. It didn't help Baylor. The Bears were unbeaten when COVID forced them to sit down. They lost soon after coming back and took a while to get back on track. Gonzaga, meanwhile, rolled on undefeated. They won all of their regular-season games by at least 10 points, a new NCAA record. Kansas earned a spot in the record books, too. In November, they were part of the AP Top 25 for the 222nd week in a row, setting a new all-time mark (but their streak ended later in the season at 231 weeks).

Most conferences held their championship tournaments, and there were more than enough teams to fill out a very strong NCAA field for both men and women. Both of those tournaments provided enough thrills to help everyone forget COVID, 40 minutes at a time.

Luka Garza

TOP AWARDS

WOODEN AND NAISMITH AWARDS

Luka Garza, IOWA
Paige Bueckers, CONNECTICUT

AP COACH OF THE YEAR

Juwan Howard, MICHIGAN
Brenda Frese, MARYLAND

FINAL MEN'S TOP 10
Coaches Poll

1. Baylor
2. Gonzaga
3. Houston
4. Michigan
5. Alabama
6. Arkansas
7. UCLA
8. Illinois
9. USC
10. Florida State

FINAL WOMEN'S TOP 10
Coaches Poll

1. Stanford
2. Arizona
3. Connecticut
4. South Carolina
5. Baylor
6. Louisville
7. North Carolina State
8. Indiana
9. Maryland
10. Texas A&M

Men's Highlights

Cunningham rose up to beat the Jayhawks.

Remember the Dons:
A long time ago, the University of San Francisco had one of the best teams in the country. Of course, it helped that **Bill Russell** played there in 1955 and 1956 (look him up—he was awesome!). In late 2020, USF was back in the headlines with a shocking November upset of No. 4 Virginia 61-60. USF had not beaten a top-five team since 1981! The Dons scored the final eight points of the game in a rally for the W.

One Night, Two Upsets:
January 12, 2021, was a night for upsets. Superstar **Cade Cunningham** (he's probably in the NBA by now) led Oklahoma State to a 75-70 win over No. 6 Kansas. On the same night, Purdue came up with shot-stuffing defense and beat No. 8 Michigan State 71-42.

Turnabout:
Michigan State did its own upsetting a few weeks later. They shook up the Big Ten race by upsetting No. 2 Michigan and No. 4 Ohio State in the same weekend. MSU had also beaten No. 5 Illinois a few days earlier. The March streak helped the Spartans make it into the NCAA tournament.

And Then There Was One:
Baylor was one of only two undefeated major teams. Then they were upset by No. 17 Kansas in late February, leaving only Gonzaga with a perfect record. The Zags ended the regular season 26–0.

Women's Highlights

Streak Snapped: No. 1 South Carolina lost its top spot and its 29-game winning streak when No. 8 North Carolina State pulled a big upset in December 2020. **Kayla Jones** led the way for the Wolfpack with 18 points in her team's surprising 54-46 win.

Top Coach: When No. 1 Stanford rolled over Pacific 104-61, coach **Tara VanDerveer** became No. 1 herself. The win was the 1,099th of her career, setting a new all-time record. She is in her 35th season at Stanford, and 42nd overall.

Ducks Go Down: No. 8 Oregon had won 27 games in a row dating back to last season. That streak ended when No. 11 UCLA beat the Ducks 73-71.

Cardinal Get Buffaloed: No. 1 Stanford lost to unranked Colorado 77-72. The Buffaloes had a losing conference record, but their tough defense shut down the mighty Cardinal. A last-play block by **Peanut Tuitele** clinched the victory. It was Stanford's first loss of the season.

Down Goes Another One: North Carolina State was ranked No. 4, so they were supposed to be pretty good. But their 74-60 victory over No. 1 Louisville on February 1 was still a big upset. The Cardinal had been 16–0 before three NC State players each scored 16 points to seal the win.

Raina Perez's NC State beat South Carolina.

Turn the Paige: Connecticut has had some great players over the years, but freshman **Paige Bueckers** might be the best. She became the first Huskies player ever with three straight 30-point games as No. 2 UConn beat No. 1 South Carolina 63-59 in overtime.

Men's NCAA Tournament

The 68 men's teams in the tournament all gathered in Indianapolis. Following COVID safety rules, they played in front of mostly empty seats. But they were watched by millions of fans on TV and online. Here are some of the key highlights.

OPENING ROUNDS

→ Nine teams seeded No. 10 and higher won on the first two days. That was one short of an all-time record!

Oral Roberts players celebrated a big upset!

→ The Big Ten sent nine teams to the tournament, the most by any conference. They did not do as well as expected. Eight of their teams lost on the way to the Sweet 16. Meanwhile, the Pac-12 had a super first weekend. Including upset wins by Oregon State and UCLA, the conference from the West was 9–1 after the first weekend.

→ The big upset was No. 15 Oral Roberts shocking No. 2 Ohio State. Kevin Obanor and Max Abmas led the way for the Golden Eagles. They had to survive a big Ohio State comeback. Then they watched a three-point shot clang away as the buzzer sounded to seal their 75-72 win. It was only the ninth 15-over-2 victory in NCAA tournament history!

→ No. 14 Abilene Christian over No. 3 Texas was nearly as big an upset. With just two seconds left, Joe Pleasant of Abilene sunk a pair of free throws. There was not enough time for Texas to get off a good shot, and the Wildcats were surprise winners 53-52.

→ The one thing everyone feared happened: VCU reported new COVID cases and had to forfeit its game against Oregon. It was a tough break for players who had worked hard all season. The No. 7 Ducks won their second game by knocking off No. 2 Iowa in another blow to the Big Ten.

→ UCLA and USC joined the Ducks in the Sweet Sixteen with big wins. USC shocked Kansas. They handed the Jayhawks one of the biggest defeats in their history, 85-51. UCLA beat Abilene Christian, ending that team's upset streak.

→ Three No. 1 seeds advanced: Gonzaga kept its season-long winning streak going; Michigan rolled over LSU; and Baylor beat Wisconsin to keep its title hopes alive.

SWEET 16

→ Five of the Sweet Sixteen teams were seeded No. 8 or higher!

→ Pac-12 rules! With surprising wins by No. 12 Oregon State and No. 11 UCLA, plus a victory by USC over fellow Pac-12er Oregon, the conference surprised most experts. USC's trip to the Elite Eight was the second in its history.

→ Arkansas barely escaped a loss to No. 15 Oral Roberts 72-70.

USC star Evan Mobley helped USC slam Kansas.

ELITE EIGHT

→ No. 1 Baylor escaped Arkansas with an 81-72 win. The Bears earned their first trip to the Final Four in 71 years!

→ No. 2 Houston ended Oregon State's upset streak with a 67-61 win.

Final Four

GONZAGA 93, UCLA 90

Wow! What an ending! This game was an instant classic. Gonzaga had not lost all season. It had won 30 games by 10 or more points. They were rolling in the tournament . . . but UCLA didn't care. The gritty Bruins played very strong defense in this national semifinal. They prevented high-scoring Gonzaga from taking a big lead. Johnny Juzang of UCLA kept nailing three-pointers and UCLA hung in. If they won, it would be one of the biggest upsets in Final Four history! The Bruins forced overtime, and then tied the game again with less than two seconds left. But that was enough time for Gonzaga star Jalen Suggs to launch a 40-foot shot that banked in at the buzzer (page 102). It was one of the most surprising and shocking baskets in NCAA history!

BAYLOR 78, HOUSTON 59

Meanwhile, in the other semifinal, the Baylor Bears had no trouble with Houston. They poured in three-pointers, grabbed tons of rebounds, and kept the Cougars from scoring. The halftime score was 45-20 Baylor, one of the biggest point differences ever in such a big game. Baylor headed to its first championship final since it won in 1948.

Suggs led the celebration after his big shot.

In your face! MaCeo Tague and his Baylor teammates shoved aside Drew Timme and Gonzaga.

Baylor Blowout!
NATIONAL CHAMPIONSHIP GAME

Maybe Gonzaga was tired after their stunning overtime defeat of UCLA. Or maybe Baylor was just much better! The Bears swarmed over the high-scoring Zags and led right from the start. It was 9-0 just a few minutes into the game, and Baylor later stretched the lead to 19 points in the first half. Gonzaga's undefeated season ended in an 86-70 loss. It was the third time that an undefeated team had lost in the championship final.

Jared Butler was the sharpshooter for Baylor, scoring 22 points, including four three-pointers. He was later named the Most Outstanding Player of the Final Four. Butler was one of five Baylor players with 10 or more points. Gonzaga's Jalen Suggs scored 22, but it was far from enough. Baylor ended a crazy NCAA season by winning the first national men's championship in school history (the women's team had won their first in 2016).

Women's NCAA Tournament

The women's teams who earned a spot in the 2021 tournament all gathered in San Antonio, Texas. Most experts said the field was more wide open than in past years. Would a No. 1 seed win it all for the 12th time in 13 seasons? Let the games begin!

Nothing could stop Caitlin Clark (right).

"What did you see? You don't need a quote from me. One kid hits her in the face and one kid hits her in the elbow."

— FORMER BAYLOR COACH KIM MULKEY ON THE FOUL THAT WASN'T CALLED

→ Upsets are a bit more unusual in women's hoops, but don't tell No. 13 Wright State. They shocked No. 4 Arkansas 66-62. It was the first 13 over 4 win in eight years.

→ Gonzaga's men's team stayed perfect. The women's team didn't. Though seeded No. 5, they were upset by Belmont 64-59 in the first round.

→ Congrats to Michigan and Indiana, which each earned their school's first-ever trip to the Sweet Sixteen. Indiana later upset No. 1 seed North Carolina State to reach the Elite Eight.

→ Connecticut overcame Baylor in an instant classic 69-67. Baylor felt a bit cheated, however. With just seconds left, **Dijonai Carrington** appeared to be fouled. But the refs didn't blow their whistles and the game ended.

→ No. 5 seed Georgia Tech trailed by 14 points to upset-minded Stephen F. Austin. But star guard **Lorela Cubaj** rallied her team to a 54-52 win.

→ Iowa's **Caitlin Clark** led the country in scoring in 2020–21. She did the same in her team's 87-72 win over Central Michigan, pouring in a game-high 23 points.

Women's Final Four

Arizona 69, Connecticut 59

Connecticut came in having won an all-time record 11 national titles. Arizona made sure they would not get another. **Aari McDonald** was the Pac-12 Player of the Year and she showed the Huskies why. She poured in 15 points in the first half as her team went up by 12. McDonald kept it up in the second half, reaching a total of 26 points. Not even superstar **Paige Bueckers** and her 18 points were enough. It will be Arizona's first time in the national championship game.

Stanford 66, South Carolina 65

No. 1 vs No. 1: Stanford had beaten the Gamecocks earlier in the season, knocking them out of the No. 1 ranking. Their rematch in the national semifinal ended the same way. **Zia Cooke** of South Carolina did her best, pouring in 25 points. In the fourth quarter, Stanford's **Haley Jones** buried a three-pointer to break a 45-45 tie. Late in the game, Jones scored on a layup that put Stanford ahead by one point. South Carolina nearly tipped in a game-winner, but it bounced off the rim.

NATIONAL CHAMPIONSHIP
STANFORD 54, ARIZONA 53

One thing was for sure: The Pac-12 would be the home of the national champ. That's because for the first time ever in the women's tournament, both finalists were from one conference. The teams had already played twice in 2021, so they knew each other well. Stanford had won both, however, and they came through again. Jones was named the Most Outstanding Player after scoring a team-high 17 points. Stanford was ahead for most of the game, but Arizona battled back to within a point. But even the heroics of McDonald, who missed a possible game-winning shot at the buzzer, were not enough for the Wildcats. Stanford became the first championship team, men or women, to win both the semifinal and the final by only one point each! It was Stanford's first national championship since way back in 1992, though they had reached ten other Final Fours since then.

Stanford's Haley Jones was the MOP!

LIGHTNING STRIKE TWICE!
Tampa Bay won its second Stanley Cup in a row in 2021 (right), defeating the Montreal Canadiens in five games. The Lightning captured the 2020 NHL championship (left), which they won while joined by 23 other teams in the COVID-created bubble. For all the details on TWO NHL seasons, get your sticks and pucks and read on!

NHL

NHL 2020: Lots of great ice hockey action . . . but no fans!

NHL 2019-20

The 2019–2020 season came to a screeching halt on March 12, 2020, when the NHL suspended play because of COVID-19. In the Eastern Conference, the Boston Bruins and their explosive goal-scorer, right wing **David Pastrňák**, were ahead of the Tampa Bay Lightning—a team that was starting to surge. But close behind them were the Washington Capitals, and the surprising Philadelphia Flyers were just one point behind the Caps.

The defending Stanley Cup champion St. Louis Blues sat atop the Western Conference, just two points ahead of the Colorado Avalanche. That team was having a breakout season thanks to the spectacular play of center **Nathan MacKinnon** and rookie defenseman **Cale Makar**. The Las Vegas Golden Knights and the Edmonton Oilers—with the league's top scorer, center **Leon Draisaitl**—were not far behind.

During the season, Capitals captain **Alexander Ovechkin** scored his 700th regular-season NHL goal, becoming the quickest to go from 600 goals to 700 (in just 154 games). Florida Panthers defenseman **Keith Yandle** became the fifth player in NHL history and the first born in America to play in 800 consecutive games. New York Rangers center **Mika Zibanejad** scored five goals in one game on March 5, including the overtime winner—something nobody had done in 14 years. Just a week later, with about a dozen games left, everyone was told to go home and stay there.

Almost three months later, the NHL was the first professional sport to announce plans to start playing again. On May 26, commissioner **Gary Bettman** said the regular season was officially over. To make room in the playoffs for teams that were surging ahead before the stop, 24 teams would start the tournament—eight more than usual. The top four teams in each conference would skip the first round of playoffs. The remaining 16 teams would face off in eight best-of-five series.

All the games would be played in two Canadian cities. Because of strict quarantine rules, travel across the Canadian-US border was difficult. Players, coaches, and staff stayed together in complexes of hotels, restaurants, and rinks called "bubbles." Everyone would be tested for COVID every day. There were no fans at any games. Instead, the giant arena scoreboards showed fans of both teams cheering from their homes.

2019–20 FINAL STANDINGS

EASTERN CONFERENCE	GAMES PLAYED*/ POINTS	WESTERN CONFERENCE	GAMES PLAYED*/ POINTS
BRUINS	70/100	BLUES	71/94
LIGHTNING	70/92	AVALANCHE	70/92
CAPITALS	69/90	GOLDEN KNIGHTS	71/86
FLYERS	69/89	OILERS	71/83
PENGUINS	69/86	STARS	69/82
HURRICANES	68/81	JETS	71/80
MAPLE LEAFS	70/81	FLAMES	70/79
BLUE JACKETS	70/81	PREDATORS	69/78
ISLANDERS	68/80	CANUCKS	69/78
RANGERS	70/79	WILD	69/77
PANTHERS	69/78	COYOTES	70/74
CANADIENS	71/71	BLACKHAWKS	70/72
SABRES	69/68	DUCKS	71/67
DEVILS	69/68	KINGS	70/64
SENATORS	71/62	SHARKS	70/63
RED WINGS	71/39		

* Because of COVID, the regular season ended when not every team had played the same number of games.

Alexander Ovechkin

2020 NHL Playoffs

Anton Khudobin and Dallas stopped Vegas.

The NHL playoffs began on August 1. All the games were played in two bubbles in Edmonton and Toronto. After the first round, the teams were reseeded, meaning the Boston Bruins, with the best record in the NHL, ended up with a fourth seed! As the playoffs went on, the teams played some great games, but only one team pulled off a huge upset. The result was an unlikely Stanley Cup Final between two American teams!

➡ Goaltender **Joonas Korpisalo** made an incredible 85 saves—an all-time NHL playoff record—as his Columbus Blue Jackets battled through five overtimes, only to lose to the Tampa Bay Lightning in Game 1 of their first-round playoff series.

➡ Vancouver Canucks goaltender **Thatcher Demko** started his first career playoff game as his team faced elimination by the Las Vegas Golden Knights. He stopped 42 shots and saved the day. Demko did even better the next game, making 48 saves and shutting out the Golden Knights in a big Vancouver win.

➡ Dallas Stars forward **Joel Kiviranta** was a last-minute addition to the lineup and became the first rookie to score a hat trick in a playoff Game 7. He completed the feat by scoring the game- and series-winning goal against the Colorado Avalanche with less than 10 minutes left in overtime.

CONFERENCE SEMIFINALS

DALLAS 4, LAS VEGAS 1

The Golden Knights came into this series as heavy favorites. The Stars had other ideas, but they needed extra time to win. The Stars clinched the series with an overtime 3-2 win in Game 5. Talk about nail-biters: Dallas won all five of its overtime games in the playoffs. This will be Dallas's first Stanley Cup Final since 2000.

TAMPA BAY 4, NY ISLANDERS 2

The Lightning continued its late-game magic. Tampa Bay won Games 4 and 6 in overtime to clinch a spot in the Final. **Anthony Cirelli** scored the game- and series-winner in overtime of Game 6. To reach its first Stanley Cup Final since 2004, Tampa Bay clinched each of its three series wins with an OT victory!

2020 Stanley Cup Final

GAME 1

Dallas 4, Tampa Bay 1

It was sort of not fair. The Stars had not played in five days, while the Lightning had wrapped up its previous series just two days before. Dallas took advantage, plus got a great game from goalie **Anton Khudobin**. He had 22 saves in the third period alone as the Dallas D held off the Lightning offense.

GAME 2

Tampa Bay 3, Dallas 2

Two power-play goals paved the way for the Lightning to even the series. Tampa scored all three of its goals in the first period and was able to hold off a Dallas comeback.

GAME 3

Tampa Bay 5, Dallas 2

The return of star and captain **Steven Stamkos** inspired the Lightning. Out with an injury since February, Stamkos did what he does best—scored! He played only five minutes, but Tampa Bay had more than enough to take a 2–1 lead in the series.

GAME 4

Tampa Bay 5, Dallas 4 (OT)

The Stars were not happy after the Lightning moved within one game of the championship. Dallas's **Jamie Benn** was called for a penalty in overtime. Tampa Bay's **Kevin Shattenkirk** then scored the game-winner on the power play. Video showed that Benn had not really tripped his opponent, as the refs ruled. The call stood, however.

GAME 5

Dallas 3, Tampa Bay 2 (2OT)

The Stars kept the Lightning from striking during two overtime periods. Meanwhile, veteran **Corey Perry** snuck in the game winner from short range more than nine minutes into the second OT. Dallas forward **Joe Pavelski** scored his 61st career playoff goal. That's the most ever by a player born in America!

GAME 6

Tampa Bay 2, Dallas 0

The Lightning won their second Stanley Cup Final by shutting out a strong Stars team in the clinching game. Goalie **Andrei Vasilevskiy** made 22 saves. Victor Hedman won the playoff MVP trophy. His 10 goals were the second most ever by a defenseman in the postseason.

Victor Hedman

NHL 2021

Rivalries were big in 2021 as the NHL rearranged itself into four divisions and only played other teams in each division. That meant the U.S. teams played each of their opponents eight times, often in extended homestands of two or more games in a row. In the all-Canadian North Division, the seven Canadian teams played each other 10 times. The new schedule kept travel down as teams dealt with COVID-19. Everything was shortened, too: Training camps opened on January 3, instead of in October. The 56-game (down from 82-game) season began just 10 days later.

Connor McDavid had an incredible season in 2021, even though it was shorter than usual.

2021 FINAL STANDINGS

WEST DIVISION	POINTS	CENTRAL DIVISION	POINTS	EAST DIVISION	POINTS	NORTH DIVISION	POINTS
AVALANCHE	82	HURRICANES	80	PENGUINS	77	MAPLE LEAFS	77
GOLDEN KNIGHTS	82	PANTHERS	79	CAPITOLS	77	OILERS	72
WILD	75	LIGHTNING	75	BRUINS	73	JETS	63
BLUES	63	PREDATORS	64	ISLANDERS	71	CANADIENS	59
COYOTES	54	STARS	60	RANGERS	60	FLAMES	55
KINGS	49	BLACKHAWKS	55	FLYERS	58	OTTAWA	51
SHARKS	49	RED WINGS	48	DEVILS	45	VANCOUVER	50
DUCKS	43	BLUE JACKETS	48	SABRES	37		

As the season unfolded, the Colorado Avalanche and New York Islanders paid off on the promise they showed last year, with Colorado finishing at the top of the league. The Florida Panthers surprised everyone by coming in second in their division, and the Montreal Canadiens squeaked into the playoffs on the last day.

Fans were slowly allowed back into arenas in the United States. In Canada, they had to wait until the playoffs to see a hockey game in person. Attendance at each arena was limited by local health orders.

A 100-point season is amazing when the hockey season is 82 games. But in this short season, it was almost beyond belief. **Connor McDavid** needed just 53 games to hit the century mark and wrapped up 2021 with 105 points. From 2000 to 2020, an average of 2.15 players reached 100 points each season; McDavid did it in a season with 26 fewer games. The Edmonton Oilers forward has reached 100 points in four of his six NHL seasons.

McDavid is half of an Oilers dynamic duo. He and **Leon Draisaitl** combined for 64 goals in the season, and Draisaitl finished second in points with 84. In 2019–20, Draisaitl was the top point-getter and McDavid was second.

Alexander Ovechkin continued his pursuit of **Wayne Gretzky's** career goal record (894), ending the season with 730. He passed Hall of Famers **Mike Gartner** and **Phil Esposito** to move up to sixth all-time in scoring. The Washington Capitals forward also passed **Brett Hull** to take over second place in lifetime power-play goals. At 269, he's just five behind all-time leader **Dave Andreychuk**.

Sidney Crosby played his 1,000th game in February—the first Pittsburgh Penguin to reach that milestone. His teammates all wore his No. 87 jersey during warm-ups. And in April, **Patrick Marleau** played his 1,768th NHL game, passing the record set by Hall of Famer **Gordie Howe**.

Bring on the Kraken!

In May 2021, the NHL's newest team, the Seattle Kraken, signed their first player, free agent forward **Luke Henman**. Then in June they named **Dave Hakstol** head coach. The expansion draft to fill out their roster was held July 21, and the Kraken will play their first NHL game at the start of the 2021–2022 season.

2021 Stanley Cup Playoffs

Joyful voices rang out in Montreal's Bell Centre on May 29. It was the first Canadian game with fans in the stands since March 10, 2020. The fans sang the anthem, O Canada, on their own before Game 6 of the Canadiens/Maple Leafs series. Those fans got an even bigger treat from their team. The bottom-seeded Montreal Canadiens weren't expected to do well in their first-round matchup against the top-seeded Toronto Maple Leafs. The Leafs took a 3–1 lead in the series, but **Carey Price's** superb goaltending and big plays by their young stars inspired the Canadiens to win the next three games and the series.

Fans in Canada were excited to be back!

The Winnipeg Jets' sweep of the Edmonton Oilers, led by **Connor McDavid**, was another first-round shocker. Price and the Canadiens continued their great play in the next round, holding the Jets to just six goals in four games and sweeping their way to the semifinals. In other divisions, superstar-led teams like the Pittsburgh Penguins and Washington Capitals were knocked out early, while well-balanced squads like the Las Vegas Golden Knights, New York Islanders, and Tampa Bay Lightning marched on to the semifinals.

STANLEY CUP SEMIFINALS

Montreal Canadiens 4
Las Vegas Golden Knights 2
The suprising Canadiens took advantage of Golden Knights' errors, got great play from their young stars, and magical goaltending from **Carey Price**. When forward **Artturi Lehkonen** punched home a pass from linemate **Philip Danault** in Game 6 overtime, Montreal reached the Stanley Cup Final for the first time since 1993.

Tampa Bay Lightning 4
New York Islanders 3
The Lightning and Islanders met for their second consecutive semifinals. It was a seesaw battle with two games going to overtime. With 2.7 seconds remaining, Islander **Ryan Pulock**'s block of an attempted game-tying shot by **Ryan McDonagh** sealed their Game 4 win. The Lightning shut out the Islanders 1-0 on **Yanni Gourde's** shorthanded goal in Game 7 to advance to the Stanley Cup Final.

2021 Stanley Cup Final

GAME 1
Tampa Bay 5, Montreal 1
Lightning defenseman **Erik Cernák** put his team on the scoreboard first, but outstanding goaltending by **Carey Price** kept the game tight over two periods. The third period belonged to Lightning forward **Nikita Kucherov**, who had a goal and two assists.

GAME 2
Tampa Bay 3, Montreal 1
The Canadiens came out flying, but the Lightning's **Anthony Cirelli** scored first. Montreal's young star **Nick Suzuki** tied it minutes later. Only heroic goaltending by **Andrei Vasilevskiy** kept the Lightning in the game. But with just 1.1 seconds left in the first period, Lightning center **Blake Coleman** made a spectacular dive, poking a **Barclay Goodrow** pass past Price to grab the lead.

GAME 3
Tampa Bay 6, Montreal 3
Lightning defenseman **Jan Rutta's** floating first-period shot over Price's shoulder was the first July goal ever scored in the NHL. **Victor Hedman's** goal less than two minutes later made him the first NHL player to score a goal in every calendar month. The goals were key to the Tampa win.

GAME 4
Montreal 3, Tampa Bay 2 (OT)
Montreal forward **Josh Anderson's** first-period goal gave the Canadiens their first

Vasilevskiy was a goal-stopping star!

lead of the series. **Barclay Goodrow** got Tampa on the scoreboard when he snapped home a shot off a nifty pass from **Ryan McDonagh**. Both teams exchanged goals in the third, and Montreal killed a four-minute penalty late in the period that extended into the overtime. Anderson was the hero when he drove hard to the net and poked home a rebound to win the game and keep Montreal's hopes alive.

GAME 5
Tampa Bay 1, Montreal 0
Lightning strikes twice! **Ross Colton's** second-period goal was the only one scored as Vasilevskiy made 22 saves to shut out the Canadiens and give his team their second Stanley Cup. Vasilevskiy's outstanding play, including a stingy 1.90 goals-against average, earned him the Conn Smythe Trophy as the playoffs MVP.

2019-20 NHL Awards

Hart Trophy
(Most Valuable Player)
LEON DRAISAITL, Edmonton

Vezina Trophy
(top goalie)
CONNOR HELLEBUYCK,
Winnipeg

Norris Trophy
(top defenseman)
ROMAN JOSI, Nashville

Ted Lindsay Award
(MVP chosen by the players)
LEON DRAISAITL, Edmonton

Calder Trophy
(rookie of the year)
CALE MAKAR, Colorado

Selke Trophy
(defensive forward)
SEAN COUTURIER, Philadelphia

Lady Byng Trophy
(sportsmanship)
NATHAN MacKINNON, Colorado

Josi was a defensive force for the Predators.

2021 NHL Awards

Hart Trophy
(Most Valuable Player)
CONNOR McDAVID,
Edmonton

Vezina Trophy
(top goalie)
MARC-ANDRÉ FLEURY, Las Vegas

Norris Trophy
(top defenseman)
ADAM FOX, NY Rangers

Ted Lindsay Award
(MVP chosen by the players)
CONNOR McDAVID,
Edmonton

Calder Trophy
(rookie of the year)
KIRILL KAPRIZOV,
Minnesota

Selke Trophy
(defensive forward)
ALEKSANDER BARKOV,
Florida

Lady Byng Trophy
(sportsmanship)
JACCOB SLAVIN, Carolina ▶

SOCCER

ANOTHER TITLE FOR BARCELONA

FC Barcelona is one of the most famous soccer clubs in the world, with trophies filling room after room at its famous stadium. In 1988, the club finally added a top-flight women's team, and in 2021, that team added to the trophy collection. Barcelona Feméni won the Women's Champions League, defeating Chelsea FC from England 4-0. It was a highlight of another busy year in soccer that saw teams battling each other as well as the COVID pandemic. But the games went on, and we've got all the news in here!

MLS Came Back!

In 2020, Major League Soccer had to pull down the nets early because of COVID. The teams played until March 8 and then took a time-out. Players and coaches headed home to be with family. However, by July, things had eased off enough that the league tried out the bubble idea, like the NBA had used. Gathering in Orlando, 24 teams headed into a monthlong tournament called MLS is Back! The league was among the earliest to return to the pitch. No fans were in the stands, but TV watchers saw a lot of great soccer action. They also witnessed the unity of all the players in showing their support of the Black Lives Matter movement before each game.

The teams were broken up into groups, with the winners of each entering a knockout tournament. The Portland Timbers and Orlando City SC made it through to the championship final. In that game, Portland's **Dario Zuparic** picked the right moment to score his first goal of the season. It gave the Timbers a late 2-1 lead that they never gave up.

MLS began the regular season on August 12. For the playoffs, teams were ranked by points per game (three for a win, one for a tie). Let's play!

Dario
Zuparic

2020 MLS HIGHLIGHTS

SUPPORTERS SHIELD
(BEST REGULAR-SEASON RECORD)
PHILADELPHIA

TOP GOAL SCORER
DIEGO ROSSI, LAFC

MVP
ALEJANDRO POZUELO,
Toronto FC

GOALIE OF THE YEAR
ANDRE BLAKE,
Philadelphia Union

NEWCOMER OF THE YEAR
LUCAS ZELARAYÁN,
Columbus Crew

MLS Playoff Highlights

* Goalie **Tim Melia** made three saves to lead Sporting Kansas City to a shootout victory in the playoff opener over San Jose.

* **Rodrigo Schlegel** is a defender for Orlando City. After a red card to the team's goalie during a penalty-kick shootout, Schlegel had to go into the net. Amazingly, he made a huge save to lead his team to a surprise win over New York City FC.

* Dallas and Portland needed 15 penalty kicks to determine a winner. **Jorge Villafaña**'s miss gave FC Dallas a huge upset over the defending conference champion Timbers.

* Even a goal by 17-year-old **Caden Clark** was not enough for the Red Bulls to beat the Crew. Columbus won 3-2 to advance to the conference semifinals.

* LAFC's **Christian Torres** was only 16 when he started the team's playoff game against Seattle. He and his teammates lost, however, 3-1.

* Nashville scored twice in extra time to beat Columbus 2-0. They'll face New England in the Eastern Conference final after the Revolution beat Orlando 3-1.

Schlegel: Defender-turned-goalie!

* In the West, Seattle kept its trophy hopes alive with a tight 1-0 win over Dallas. Minnesota continued its strong postseason with a 3-0 win over Sporting Kansas City.

MLS Cup 2020

CONFERENCE CHAMPIONSHIPS

East: Columbus 1, New England 0

Columbus headed back to its third MLS Cup after this win. Brazilian defender **Artur de Lima** powered in a left-footed shot after a perfect pass from **Jonathan Mensah**. The No. 8–seed Revolution's surprise run through the playoffs ended a game short.

West: Seattle 3, Minnesota 2

In a game that had one of the most thrilling endings in MLS history, defending champ Seattle scored three goals in the final 15-plus minutes to shock the Wild 3-2. Minnesota had gone ahead thanks to goals from **Emanuel Reynoso** and **Bakaye Dibassy**. **Will Bruin** got the Sounders's first goal at 75 minutes. **Raúl Ruidíaz** tied the game after a corner kick with just a minute left. In extra time, a minute before the final whistle, **Gustav Svensson** flicked in a header for the winning goal. Seattle headed to its fourth MLS Cup in five seasons.

MLS CUP 2020

Columbus 3, Seattle 0

The Crew almost left their home city a few years ago. That made this MLS Cup title very special. They gave the home fans a thrill with a solid victory to win their second MLS championship (the first came back in 2008). **Lucas Zelarayán** scored the first of his two goals in the 25th minute. **Derrick Etienne Jr.** banged in goal number two, before Zelarayán capped off the night with a left-footed blast. Seattle must have left all its magic back in the semifinal!

Lucas Zelarayán slipped in this goal in the MLS Cup.

They'll always be the first champs of the first Challenge Cup: Congrats to the Houston Dash!

NWSL 2020

The First Ones Back!

The National Women's Soccer League (NWSL) was the first team sport to get back in action after the pandemic started in spring 2020. Eight teams took part in the Challenge Cup tournament in Utah in late June and most of July. The players all stayed together in a "soccer village" and played the games in front of empty seats. The teams battled through round-robin games that set the seeding for a knockout tournament. The Houston Dash came out on top in the championship game, defeating the Chicago Red Stars 2-0.

COVID prevented NWSL from having a full league schedule later in the year. Still, the players showed the same creativity they had shown in Utah. The Fall Series set up groups of three teams that played a series of four games each. They piled up points, and the Portland Thorns came out on top,

followed by the Houston Dash. Money raised during the event went to charities of the winning team's choice!

The Challenge Cup was such a hit that NWSL repeated the event in 2021. The Thorns outlasted Gotham FC in a penalty-kick shootout to win the event. Then came the NWSL regular season. However, the championship was held after our book was printed. Help us out. Fill in the winner and runner-up for the 2021 NWSL season here!

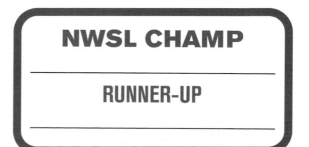

NWSL CHAMP

_____

RUNNER-UP

_____

Champions League 2020

Kingsley Coman
of Liverpool

Like everything else in sports in 2020, this important European club tournament had to make a few adjustments. The final rounds were postponed until August (usually they are held in June). The final eight teams were sent to live and play in a "bubble" formed in Porto, Portugal. Most Champions League playoff games are also two matches each; the winner moves on based on total goals in the two games. Because of the bubble, the playoffs were one game each.

Several teams advanced farther than they ever had, showing the growing strength of many European leagues.

In the first semifinal, Paris Saint-Germain (PSG) won to earn its first Champions League final spot. They beat RB Leipzig from Germany, who was making its own first semifinal appearance. Bayern Munich won the other semi, knocking off upset-minded Lyon from France 3-0. Bayern was clearly the team to beat in the final. Not only were they on a 28-game unbeaten streak, but they had beaten mighty Barcelona 8-2 in the quarterfinals!

In its 11th Champions League final, the powerful German team beat PSG 1-0 on a goal by **Kingsley Coman** (who used to play for PSG!). That gave Bayern six all-time Champions League crowns.

Champions League 2021

BEST YEAR FOR AMERICANS

A record seven American players took part in Champions League games during the early part of the playoffs, a good sign that US soccer power is rising. Chelsea's **Christian Pulisic** became the first American player to score in a Champions League semifinal when he put in the first goal of his team's 2-1 win over Real Madrid. He sealed the team's spot in the final with a brilliant assist in the second leg of the semifinal. In the final, Pulisic became the first American man to win a Champions League title. Three American women had beat him to it, though!

MEN'S FINAL

Chelsea 1, Manchester City 0

The final Champions League match is always set for a single city way ahead of the event. This game was originally planned for Istanbul. Once two English teams made it to the final, and because of ongoing COVID issues in Turkey, the game was moved to nearby Porto, Portugal. Though Manchester City was favored, they could not find the back of the net. Chelsea's **Kai Havertz** scored just before halftime, and the Blues made the goal stand up.

Aitana Bonamati led the way for Barça.

WOMEN'S FINAL

Barcelona 4, Chelsea 0

Chelsea did not do as well in the women's final. The game could not have gotten off to a better start for Barcelona. Only 33 seconds into the match, Chelsea knocked in an own goal! Over the next 30-plus minutes, Barcelona just poured it on. They scored on a penalty kick, then goals by **Aitana Bonamatí** and **Caroline Hansen** made it 4-0 before halftime! Chelsea could not come back in the second half, and that's how the final score stood. Barcelona switched into the club's famous red-and-gold-striped shirts for a joyous celebration.

Pulisic (left) celebrates his historic win.

EPL 2020

Liverpool...Finally!

Captain Jordan Henderson (center) celebrates Liverpool's first Premier League title.

By the late summer of 2020, Liverpool was *really* tired of waiting! The famous English team was once the best in Europe. They had won 18 league championships in their 128 years of history. But they had not won the English top league since 1990. As the 2019–20 English Premier League season sped along, it was clear that Liverpool's streak was probably going to end. The men in red were cruising through the season, piling up win after win. By early March, they had earned 82 points, an incredible 25 ahead of second-place Manchester City.

Then, of course . . . COVID!

Sports stopped for a while, and it was exactly 100 days before the EPL could safely return to the field. The teams played without fans in the stands in order to wrap up the remaining games. (There are no playoffs in the EPL; the team with the most total points wins.)

Liverpool thumped Crystal Palace 4-0 to earn three big points. Then they watched on TV as Manchester City played Chelsea. A loss by City would clinch the title for Liverpool. When the final whistle blew, the players jumped around and high-fived each other, piling up around their coach, **Jürgen Klopp**. It was not the fan-filled celebration they wanted, but the championship feeling was just as sweet. They had set a new record with 24 straight wins at home and tied an EPL record with 32 victories.

EPL 2021
Man City Wins!

Here's a combination for success in soccer: don't give up many goals and score more than anyone else. Seems simple, right? But it's hard to do in real life. In the 2020–21 Premier League, Manchester City followed that formula to perfection. The men in light blue won the league with 86 points, thanks in large part to a 15-match winning streak from December 1 to March 7.

On the defensive side, center back **Rúben Dias** led the way. The team allowed only 32 goals in 38 matches, including 19 shutouts.

On offense, the team led the EPL with 83 goals. In a show of the team's depth, 14 different City players found the back of the net. Only two of them—**Ilkay Gündogan** and **Raheem Sterling**—scored 10 or more. The key to the City attack, though, was former player of the year **Kevin De Bruyne** (pictured). The Belgian midfielder was a passing wizard, racking up 12 assists along with six key goals.

The winning formula gave City its third Premier League title in the past four seasons.

Goalie Goal!

With just seconds left in the game, Liverpool was tied with West Bromwich. Without a win in the game, the Reds would probably end up out of the 2022 Champions League. So in desperation, goalkeeper **Alisson Becker** ran up to take part in a corner kick. Incredibly, he nodded in a goal, the first ever scored by a keeper in Liverpool's 126-year history. Teammates mobbed him in thanks for the season-saving shot. "It's the best goal I've ever scored," he said after the 2-1 win. "Actually, it's the only goal!"

Colombia goalie David Ospina came up big in a penalty shootout with Uruguay.

Copa America ~~2020~~ 2021

COVID pushed this championship of South American national teams from 2020 to 2021. It also moved it from its original sites in Colombia and Argentina to Brazil.

Some teams were affected by COVID outbreaks, but the games went on! And fans around the world saw some amazing soccer action that included top teams such as Brazil and Argentina. All ten teams in CONMEBOL, which is the soccer federation in South America, took part in two groups of five teams. Only two teams were knocked out after group play, Bolivia and Venezuela.

GROUP PLAY HIGHLIGHTS

* Argentina won Group A. Its superstar **Lionel Messi** showed why he is one of the best in the world with a beautiful free-kick goal in a win over Chile.

* Paraguay was a surprise second place in Group A after beating Chile for the third straight time in Copa America, dating back to 2007!

* Venezuela needed a tie or a win in its final game against Peru—and they lost 1-0 and were out.

* As expected, Brazil looked dominant. It earned the most points in group-stage games, with 10. Superstar **Neymar Jr.** scored two goals.

* Colombia overcame Uruguay in penalty kicks to advance to the semifinals to face mighty Argentina. Brazil knocked off a hard-fighting Chile team and will play surprising Peru in the other semi.

SEMIFINAL MATCHES

BRAZIL 1, PERU 0

Brazil heads to its seventh Copa America final after beating Peru. The great striker Neymar had an assist on the only goal, struck home by **Lucas Paquetá** in the 34th minute. Peruvian goalie **Pedro Gallese** did all he could, making several big saves, but his teammates could not sore. After the game, Neymar said, "I want Argentina in the final. I am cheering for them because I have many friends there. In the final, Brazil will win."

ARGENTINA 1, COLOMBIA 1
PKs: Argentina 3-2

Neymar got his wish. It took penalty kicks, but Messi and Argentina slipped past Colombia. **Lautaro Martínez** scored in just the seventh minute, but Colombia got even in the 61st thanks to a goal by **Luis Díaz**. Even the great Messi could not find the net again and the upset-minded Colombia team had a shot in penalties. But they missed two of their first three attempts (Messi made his) and Argentina won.

Neymar Jr.

Messi goes for a championship flight!

CHAMPIONSHIP MATCH
ARGENTINA 1, BRAZIL 0

Messi is clearly one of the best players of all time. But he had never led his national team to a major championship. That changed in this game. **Ángel Di María** scored in the first half on a great chip over the goalie's head. Argentina then held on during wave after wave of Brazil attacks. When the final whistle view, Messi's teammates tossed him in the air in celebration. He finally had his big trophy.

European Championship ~~2020~~ 2021

Like its South American counterpart, the championship among Europe's national teams was moved from 2020 to 2021. The event is one of the most famous and popular on the world soccer calendar, and fans everywhere were excited that the games were finally played.

The top 24 teams on the continent qualified. After group play, the top 16 teams made it into knockout playoffs. Here are some highlights from the group-stage and quarterfinal games:

✳ In Denmark's first game, star **Christian Ericksen** suddenly collapsed. Doctors rushed to his side and had to save his life after a heart attack. Shocked fans and players waited for good news, which came quickly when Ericksen called his team that day from the hospital.

✳ Wales pushed into the knockouts thanks to a big win over Turkey. **Aaron Ramsey** scored first for the Red Dragons before **Connor Roberts** added an extra-time goal to make it 2-0.

✳ **Patrick Schick** looped a shot from his own half high over the Scottish goalie's head for the goal of the tournament (so far!).

✳ Spain scored twice in extra time to beat Croatia in the round of 16 after Croatia had tied the game in the 93rd minute.

✳ Still inspired by Ericksen, Denmark beat Wales 4-0 to reach the quarterfinals.

✳ Round of 16 shockers: Switzerland upset France in penalty kicks! The Czech Republic surprised the Netherlands!

Surprising Switzerland celebrated after knocking out defending-champion France.

Harry Kane led England to the final.

ENGLAND 2, DENMARK 1

A great free kick by **Mikkel Damsgaard** gave Denmark a first-half lead before England tied it thanks to a Denmark own goal (which would have been buried by **Raheem Sterling** anyway!). In extra time, **Harry Kane** smacked in a blocked penalty kick to put England ahead, and a tired Denmark could not answer. England headed toward its first tournament final of any kind since 1966.

CHAMPIONSHIP MATCH
ITALY 1, ENGLAND 1
Italy Wins in PKs, 3-2

The dream for England died when Italy's **Gianluigi Donnarumma** blocked **Bukayo Saka**'s penalty kick. That ended a shootout the teams needed after 120 minutes. England scored only two minutes into the game on a great left-footed shot by **Luke Shaw**. Italy tied the score in the second half when **Leonardo Bonnucci** knocked the ball in after a scramble. The championship for Italy was its first in Europe since 1968.

Jorginho of Italy

SEMIFINAL MATCHES
ITALY 1, SPAIN 1
PKs: Italy 3, Spain 2

After a scoreless first half, Italy's **Federico Chiesa** curled in a beautiful shot around Spanish keeper **Unai Simón**. It looked like that would carry Italy to the final until Spain finally cracked the Italian defensive wall. **Alvaro Morata** slipped in a left-footed shot in the 80th minute to tie the score. Neither team could score again, though, and the game ended with a penalty-kick shootout. Spain missed one and had another blocked. Italy had only one blocked, and **Jorginho** put his in to clinch the victory.

SheBelieves Cup 2021

The SheBelieves Cup has become a tough test for the world's best women's soccer teams. In 2021, it served as a sort of tune-up for the Summer Olympics—and perhaps a preview of the 2023 Women's World Cup?

The US national team faced Argentina, Canada, and Brazil. In the opening match, **Rose Lavelle** scored after coming off the bench to beat Canada 1-0 in the toughest match of the tournament for the US. In the US's 2-0 win over Brazil, **Lindsey Horan** assisted on goals by **Christen Press** and **Megan Rapinoe**.

The Americans needed only a tie in the final match against Argentina to win the Cup. They did more than that, piling up goal after goal for a 6-0 rout. Rapinoe scored the first two goals, followed by one from all-time great **Carli Lloyd**. Veteran **Kristie Mewis** made it 4-0. In the second half, **Alex Morgan** scored for the first time since taking time off to have a

The US team welcomed back star Alex Morgan.

daughter. Press scored on a header to wrap up the scoring and the trophy.

It was the fourth time the US has won the tournament, and the second season in a row. The team also stretched its unbeaten streak to 37 games!

2021 GOLD CUP

The Gold Cup is held every two years to determine the best team in CONCACAF. That is one of soccer's international regions and includes North and Central America and the Caribbean. Since 2002, the champion has been either Mexico or the United States. In 2021, the US sent a very young team but fought hard. They beat Qatar (a guest in the tournament) in the semifinal; goalie **Matt Turner** made several huge saves to seal the win. Three times in recent Gold Cups, the US had lost to Mexico in the final. After the Qatar win, the Americans once again faced their biggest rival in the championship game. The game almost went to a penalty-kick shootout, but **Miles Robinson** headed in a goal in the 117th minute. The US won its seventh Gold Cup 1-0.

What a Game!

The US men's national soccer team and the Mexican soccer team are neighbors . . . and longtime rivals. The two teams have met for years in intense battles. The rivalry continued in the 2021 Nations League, a mini-tournament of teams from North and Central America. The championship game, played in Denver, turned into one of the most memorable and hard-fought in the long history of the series.

The game could not have started worse for the Americans. Less than two minutes into the game, **Joe Corona** intercepted a bad pass and drove a shot into the US goal past **Ethan Horvath**. Mexico was up 1-0. It was almost 2-0, but a Mexican goal was taken off due to offside. Right after that, **Gio Reyna** scored to tie it 1-1. A speedy Mexican sub, **Diego Lainez**, smacked in a left-footed shot to give his team the lead. The US was not done, and **Weston McKennie** smashed in a header to tie the score. The two teams needed extra time to find a winner. In the game's 109th minute, US star **Christian Pulisic** was fouled in the penalty box. He buried the penalty kick and it looked like the US had won. But a handball led to a penalty kick for Mexico. If it went in, the game would be tied and probably end with a shootout. But Horvath made a miraculous save. Then, due to injuries and some wild fans on the field, the game needed more than 10 minutes of extra time before the final whistle. In the end, Horvath's save (below) was the difference, and the US won an instant classic.

NASCAR

LONG SHOT WINNER
Michael McDowell got the 2021 NASCAR season off to a wild start when he zipped past a last-lap crash to win the Daytona 500, his first Cup Series victory (that's his car under the yellow arrow). Brad Kesolowski and Joey Logano tangled bumpers. McDowell was right behind and managed to avoid the crash. He zoomed into the lead for the first time and held on to zip under the checkered flag. It was the start of another great NASCAR season. Read on to look back at 2020 and see what else 2021 had in store.

Kevin Harvick was on top of his car and on top of the regular season standings in 2020.

NASCAR 2020

If there was one thing clear about the 2020 NASCAR regular season, it was that having a name that started with H was the way to go. The other thing that was clear is that every race and every lap counts . . . and that winning early isn't enough. You have to win late.

During the regular season, heading into the Chase for the Cup playoffs, **Kevin Harvick** won seven races while **Denny Hamlin** won six, putting them miles ahead of the competition. See, H's did well!

All of NASCAR took a long time-out in March and April due to COVID-19. Races began again on May 17 with a fan-free race at Darlington. Not surprisingly, Harvick won that one to keep his early hot

Empty seats watched most races in 2020.

7-Time Champ Retires

The final race at Phoenix in 2020 was also the last race in the career of one of the all-time greats. Jimmie Johnson, tied for first with seven season championships, rolled off the track for the final time. He was the first driver from outside the South to win the title when he ended up on top. He won five in a row from 2006 through 2010, the longest streak ever, and then won again in 2013 and 2016. Johnson is not leaving racing, though. In 2021, he'll drive road courses in IndyCar!

CHASE FOR THE CUP!
2020 FINAL STANDINGS

1. Chase ELLIOTT
2. Brad KESELOWSKI
3. Joey LOGANO
4. Denny HAMLIN
5. Kevin HARVICK
6. Alex BOWMAN
7. Martin TRUEX JR.
8. Kyle BUSCH
9. Ryan BLANEY
10. Kurt BUSCH

streak going. Fans were allowed to trickle in to races starting in New Hampshire in August. Brad Keselowski won that race, one of three checkered flags he had in the regular season.

Harvick took over with a dominating second half, including back-to-back wins in one weekend in Michigan as NASCAR packed in doubleheaders.

As the regular season wrapped up, six former NASCAR champions were part of the playoff field, including Harvick, the 2014 winner. Cole Custer was the only rookie to break through into the final 16. Matt DiBenedetto made the field in his sixth season. Joey Logano came into the playoffs on a hot streak, with wins in two of the final four regular-season races. Defending champ Martin Truex Jr. also headed into September on a hot streak, with eight straight top-four finishes, but no victories. "I feel like we are right there on the edge of winning a couple in a row," said Truex.

But it was a strong late finish by Chase Elliott that helped him capture his first NASCAR season championship. He was the last winner standing!

2020 CHASE FOR THE CUP!

As usual, the tight-packed racing at Talladega turned this race into a demolition derby!

PLAYOFFS

ROUND OF 16

DARLINGTON: Gee, surprise. Kevin Harvick won. NASCAR's hottest driver, top-ranked in the playoff field, earned his spot in the next round right off the bat. He squeaked to victory by less than a second over Austin Dillon.

RICHMOND: Brad Keselowski joined Harvick in the next round with a dominating victory. He zoomed over the finish line more than 2.5 seconds ahead of Martin Truex Jr. Denny Hamlin joined the two winners in the next round with his 12th-place finish—that's what you get for entering the playoffs so far ahead!

BRISTOL: Ho, hum, another win by Harvick. He won his ninth race of the season by preventing Kyle Busch from passing him on the final laps.

OUT: William Byron, Cole Custer, Ryan Blaney, Matt DiBenedetto

ROUND OF 8

LAS VEGAS: The Busch brothers grew up in Las Vegas, but until this race, Kurt Busch had never won at the Vegas track. He ended a 21-loss streak with a win that sent him into the next round of the playoffs.

TALLADEGA: This was not a race, it was a test of survival. The superspeedway saw 13 crashes, more than other race this season. All the wrecks added 12 laps to the race, which was won by (who else?) Hamlin. He snuck around two other cars on the last lap to win his seventh race of the year. Only six of the remaining 12 Chase drivers even managed to finish the race!

CHARLOTTE: On the unusual "roval" course (a mix of road course and traditional oval), Chase Elliott came out ahead, clinching a spot in the next round. Kyle Busch finished 30th, which means he wouldn't get a chance to defend his 2019 NASCAR title.

OUT: Kyle Busch, Austin Dillon, Clint Bowyer, Aric Almirola

FINAL ROUND

KANSAS: Joey Logano held off a fast-charging Kevin Harvick for the win and a spot in the final four. It was the first victory for Logano since March, and couldn't have come at a better time.

TEXAS: When the race is on the line, NASCAR teammates don't let up. Kyle Busch finished less than a half second ahead of fellow Joe Gibbs Racing driver Truex. That kept Truex from clinching a spot in the championship final four.

MARTINSVILLE: In the last race before the final in Phoenix, three spots were still up for grabs. Thrilling his many fans, Chase Elliott grabbed one of them with a victory on this famous short track in Virginia. It was his first win here—that topped his famous dad, Bill, who never won at Martinsville in 45 tries! Meanwhile, winning nine races was not enough for Harvick, who fell just one point short of the final four. Keselowski and Hamlin squeaked in ahead of him for the other two spots.

OUT: Kevin Harvick, Alex Bowman, Kurt Busch, and Martin Truex Jr.

CHAMPIONSHIP RACE

PHOENIX: Like father, like son! For the third time, a father-son pair claimed NASCAR season championships. Chase Elliott roared to victory in the season finale at Phoenix to win the 2020 season title. His father won in 1988. Chase had to work hard for his big win. A victory at Martinsville a week earlier let him squeeze into the final four. He earned the pole at Phoenix but then was shocked when a prerace inspection found something wrong with his car. He had to move all the way to the back of the 39-car field. Still, he roared to the front and took the lead for good with 43 laps remaining. In fifth place was seven-time champion Jimmie Johnson, who was in his final NASCAR race.

Elliott hoists the winning hardware!

Other NASCAR Champs

Truck Series

Making the right choice is sometimes as important as being the fastest. **Brett Moffitt** was leading with just three laps to go in the Truck Series final race in Arizona. Then a crash put the race under yellow-flag caution. His rival, **Sheldon Creed**, decided to risk putting on new tires for the sprint to the finish. Moffitt didn't. In overtime, Creed's fresh tires helped him whiz past Moffitt for his first Truck Series championship.

XFINITY SERIES

The champion of the Xfinity Series also benefited from new tires. But it was his surprising pass late in an overtime restart that made **Austin Cindric** the champ. He roared past teammate **Noah Gragson** and squeaked under the checkered flag just 0.162 seconds ahead. It was Cindric's sixth race win of the season, but his first overall season title.

NASCAR 2021 Notes

Early Season Action

NASCAR got 2021 off to a very polite start. The sport usually sees lots of me-first driving, as racers will do anything to win. But at first, they looked like they were taking turns nicely! Six different drivers won the first six races, each automatically earning a spot in the Chase for the Cup playoffs. For the first time since 1950, the first two events were won by first-time winners! **Michael McDowell** won the Daytona 500. The next week, **Christopher Bell** took his first checkered flag at the road-course event at Daytona. The pattern continued through April, as nine different drivers won at least one race out of the first 10 events.

Marvelous Martin

Former champion **Martin Truex Jr.** was the first winner to break the pattern in 2021. He won at Martinsville after winning in Phoenix. He kept up his trips to Victory Lane as the first driver to win three races in the season. At Darlington, he dueled **Joey Logano** on the final lap, before pulling away to win by only 2.5 seconds. That put him into the postseason playoff, of course, but also put him in first place through the end of May.

Back to the Dirt

Before superspeedways and tight asphalt ovals, NASCAR races were held on dirt tracks. Drivers learned to slide through turns on the bumpy, slick surfaces. At the Bristol race in March 2021, NASCAR jumped into a time machine. The half-mile track in Tennessee with 2,300 truckloads of dirt, which was all on top of a layer of sawdust. The drivers went back to their roots amid dust clouds and flying clods. Logano finished in first place and was thrilled. "How about Bristol on dirt? This is an incredible, unbelievable race track," he said. The race will be repeated in 2022; believe it or not, the same dirt will be stored to use again!

Time to use the windshield wipers! NASCAR returned to its dirt-covered roots at Bristol.

OTHER MOTOR SPORTS

ONE FOR THE RECORD BOOKS

Lewis Hamilton roars past his cheering teammates after clinching his record-tying seventh Formula 1 driver's championship. The British speedster also set marks for all-time race victories in a shortened F1 season. Read about all the world motor sports action inside!

After an early-season delay, it was off to the races for Formula 1, here in action in Russia.

Formula 1 2020

Because of COVID-19, the 2020 Formula 1 season stayed in the garage for a while. Scheduled to start in March, the drivers waited until July to hit the track. Once they started, the action was high speed and high drama.

For the past several seasons, Great Britain's **Lewis Hamilton** has dominated the sport. So as much as things were different in 2020, that fact remained the same. After Hamilton's Mercedes teammate **Valtteri Bottas** beat him in Austria to

Valtteri Bottas tried to catch his Mercedes teammate, Lewis Hamilton.

Not even a blown tire could slow down Hamilton's race for another title.

open the season, Hamilton won five of the next six races. In winning the British Grand Prix in early August, the five-time F1 champ showed that he is so good that he only needs three tires to win a race. Leading on the last lap of the British Grand Prix, the left front tire of his Formula 1 car popped! No problem for this driver. Hamilton nursed his car across the finish line to win at Silverstone for the seventh time in his amazing career. It was his 87th career win overall.

Hamilton kept at it. During qualifying for the race in Italy, he pushed his Mercedes to a speed of 164.267 miles per hour (264.362 kph). It was the all-time record for fastest lap at the famous Monza track. Of course, the way his season was going—he didn't win that race! **Pierre Gasly** won his first-ever F1 title after Hamilton suffered a penalty that pushed him back to seventh. Still, Hamilton stretched his overall season lead to more than 60 points.

Penalties crushed Hamilton's chances in the Russian Grand Prix, too. One race short of the all-time record for wins, Hamilton was pushed back in the pack for doing illegal practice runs. Still, he finished third behind teammate Valtteri Bottas.

Hamilton kept charging, however, with history in his sights. At the Eifel Grand Prix in Germany, Hamilton roared to victory. It was his seventh of the 2020 season and

the 91st of his career. That put him in a tie with the great German driver **Michael Schumacher** for most career race victories ever! Hamilton broke the tie in Portugal the next week. Zooming past Bottas on the 20th lap, Hamilton held on to become the all-time winningest Formula 1 driver. His dad and other family members were on hand for the big celebration! All that was left was to bring home the driver's championship, and he did that with a win in Turkey in November. That tied him with Schumacher with seven career Formula 1 championships! (For the record, he has won the title in 2008, 2014, 2015, 2017, 2018, 2019, and 2020.) Hamilton added one more race in Bahrain to wrap up the 2020 season . . . better late than never!

2020 FORMULA 1 TOP DRIVERS

PLACE/DRIVER/TEAM	POINTS
1. **Lewis Hamilton**, Mercedes	347
2. **Valtteri Bottas**, Mercedes	223
3. **Max Verstappen**, Red Bull	214
4. **Sergio Perez**, Racing Point	125
5. **Daniel Ricciardo**, Renault	119

IndyCar 2020

IndyCar waved the red flag on the 2020 season in March, just before the first scheduled race. But the circuit put together a plan for safety off the track, and the action on the track got the green flag on June 6. No fans were in the stands, but the drivers were in their seats and the action was, as usual, fast and furious!

Scott Dixon roared out of the starting grid with wins in the first three races of the shortened season, including a July 4 title at the Indianapolis Motor Speedway. Dixon won only one of the next eight races, however, as a variety of drivers took their turns waving the checkered flag. Defending champ **Josef Newgarden** got wins at Iowa and Gateway near St. Louis.

The famous Indy 500 was finally held on August 23. More than 300,000 empty seats watched one of the oddest finishes in the race's 104-year history. With just five laps to go, a crash brought out a yellow flag. IndyCar officials decided not to force a restart and the cars limped home at about 50 miles an hour. **Takuma Sato** was in the lead when the yellow went out and he stayed there to cross the finish line slower than your family car goes on the freeway!

After a delay to the season, Scott Dixon kept up his drive on the record books.

INDY 500 '21

Brazilian star **Helio Castroneves** became the fourth driver ever to win four Indy 500s. He waited until two laps from the end to make his move, then zoomed past leader **Álex Palou** into first place. After zipping past the brick-covered finish line, he thrilled fans by climbing the fence to celebrate (left). No wonder his nickname is "Spider-Man"! The more than 135,000 fans at the race were the largest crowd for a sporting event since the COVID-19 pandemic closed most such things in March 2020. Castroneves previously won the world's most famous race in 2001, 2002, and 2009.

Heading into October, Dixon's hot start had kept him atop the season standings. Newgarden was close behind. In a surprising third place was **Pato O'Ward** of Mexico, who had not won a race but had eight top-10 finishes.

When the crazy season finally reached the last race in Florida, Newgarden had one more shot to overtake Dixon. He would have to win the race and have Dixon finish tenth or worse. Amid a series of crashes—and even rain—Newgarden did his job. He avoided trouble and roared to the checkered flag. Dixon, however, kept pace and finished third. That gave the New Zealand native enough points to win his sixth IndyCar season championship.

2020 INDYCAR FINAL STANDINGS

PLACE/DRIVER	POINTS
1 Scott Dixon	537
2 Josef Newgarden	521
3 Colton Herta	421
4 Pato O'Ward	416
5 Will Power	396
6 Graham Rahal	377
7 Takuma Sato	348
8 Simon Pagenaud	339
9 Alexander Rossi	317
10 Ryan Hunter-Reay	315

Drag Racing

TOP FUEL: **Steve Torrence** was tops again in Top Fuel. He won his third straight national championship driving the long, skinny, huge-wheeled speed monsters. Only **Doug Kalitta** had a shot at topping the season leader, but Kalitta lost early at Las Vegas, handing Torrence the trophy. One of his wins on the way to the title was over his teammate—and father!—**Billy Torrence**.

FUNNY CAR: The DSR team drivers won all 11 of the Funny Car competitions held in 2020. **Matt Hagan** outlasted all of them to make the final race at the NHRA Finals in Las Vegas. That gave him enough points to earn his third season championship in drag racing's second fastest event.

PRO STOCK: When **Jason Line** lost at Las Vegas in a qualifying round, **Erica Enders** won the whole season. Line's loss meant that he could not pile up enough points to overcome Enders, who had arrived in Vegas leading the season. The trophy was her second in a row and fourth overall.

PRO STOCK MOTORCYCLE:

Matt Smith guided his high-speed bike to a spot in the Las Vegas finals. That was all he needed to wrap up a dominant 2020 season with the title. It was his fourth championship, which is tied for third-most all-time. It was a nice bounceback for him after losing the 2019 title due to a mechanical problem in his final race.

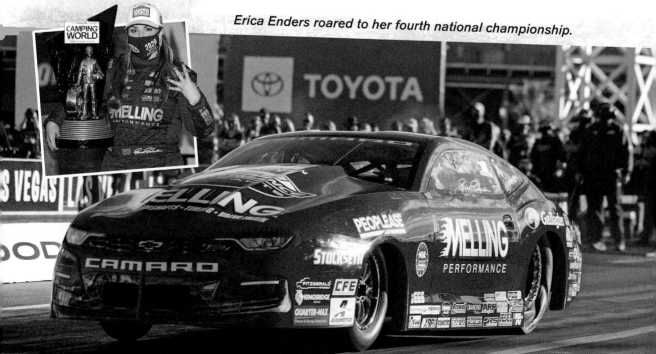

Erica Enders roared to her fourth national championship.

Motorcycle Racing

Zach Osborne

2020 MOTOCROSS

For the first time since 2016, AMA Motocross had a new season 450 champion. **Eli Tomac** had won three straight and had his eye on No. 4, but **Zach Osborne** had other ideas. A hot start by Osborne with three wins in four races had everyone playing catchup. He won one other race but had a series of high finishes to keep piling up the points. In the final at Las Vegas, he rode safely and finished sixth. Those points put him in first place for the season. It was his first title, and at 31, he was the oldest motocross champ ever. In the 250 class, France's **Dylan Ferrandis** finished in the top three in eight of nine races to win his first season title, too.

2021 SUPERCROSS

If you want to go out a winner . . . go out a winner! In the final race of the 2021 Supercross season at Las Vegas, **Cooper Webb** only needed to finish 19th or better to earn enough points to clinch the season title. He did better than that! Near the end of the race, Webb nudged around former champ **Ken Roczen** to move into second place. Then he found leader **Chase Sexton**, chased him down, and zoomed past. A moment later, Webb soared over the final jump, the race winner and the champ all in one! It was Webb's second AMA Supercross national championship in the past three years.

Cooper Webb

GOLF

CROWD FAVORITE
Phil Mickelson rolled in this putt to finish off his victory in the 2021 PGA Championship at Kiawah Island, South Carolina. "Lefty" defied the odds by winning his sixth career major in May 2021, just one month short of his 51st birthday.

2020 Majors

It was strange to watch the men's majors played with no fans lining the course. In fact, the British Open was not played at all. It marked the first time since World War II that the event was cancelled. Still, the majors that were played provided golf fans with some, well . . . major thrills.

PGA CHAMPIONSHIP: In August, **Collin Morikawa** blasted a 295-yard drive to the green of the par-4 16th hole at TPC Harding Park in San Francisco. He rolled in the seven-foot putt for an eagle that gave him the lead. Two holes later, he had won his first major championship. He was also the first player ever to have four rounds in the 60s in a major in his first attempt.

US OPEN: Boom! That's the sound of one of **Bryson DeChambeau's** monster drives. It's also the sound of the impact of his long-hitting style of play on golf. He combined huge drives with great putting to win the US Open in September for his

$15M

The FedEx Cup isn't a major tournament—it's a season-long chase to be the best golfer on the PGA Tour—but it has grown to be a really big deal since its debut in 2007. In 2020, American **Dustin Johnson** won the FedEx Cup for the first time. His victory in the season-ending Tour Championship meant he got to take home the FedEx Cup trophy—and a cool $15 million!

DeChambeau's hard work paid off.

first major championship. DeChambeau had spent a year adding power and muscle, and his hard work paid off with a six-shot win at Winged Foot Golf Club in New York.

MASTERS: The event, traditionally held in April, was moved to November. The result made history. **Dustin Johnson** set an all-time Masters record with a score of 20 under par while winning his first green jacket. He won by five strokes, one of the most dominant wins in years. Australia's **Cameron Smith** finished second with a record four rounds in the 60s.

2021 Men's Golf Notes

Ace Finish

Sergio García had a highlight shot at the WGC Match Play tournament in Austin, Texas, in March 2021. In match play, golfers compete one-on-one instead of against the entire field. García and **Lee Westwood** faced a sudden-death playoff in their match. On the fourth extra hole, a 160-yard par-3, Westwood put the ball 26 feet from the hole, which looked safe for a par. García stepped up and launched a nine-iron high in the air. It landed just a foot or two past the hole, then spun back into the cup. A walk-off hole-in-one!

A Round . . . and Around

Playing 9 or 18 holes of golf in a day is no big deal, right? Well, how about 252! That's what Swiss golfer **Jürg Randegger** did at a course in Niederbüren, Switzerland, in June 2021. Randegger set a Guinness World Record for the most holes played in less than 12 hours. He completed 14 rounds in 11 hours and 22 minutes, walking 57 miles.

Homa at Home

When he was a kid, **Max Homa** and his dad went to watch the PGA pros many times at the Riviera Country Club in Los Angeles. He grew up not far away and loved seeing the big stars play there. He never imagined that one day he'd be the champion! In February 2021, however, Homa rolled in a short par putt on the second playoff hole to beat **Tony Finau** and win the Genesis Invitational at Riviera.

Real Pressure

Though he was only 24, **Will Zalatoris** surprised fans with his calm play, good enough for a surprise second-place finish at the 2021 Masters. Less than two weeks later, though, the pressure got to the PGA Tour rookie. That's when he proposed marriage to his girlfriend, Caitlin. "I was more nervous on one knee than I was on eighteen at Augusta, there's no question about that," said Zalatoris. "But she said, 'Yes,' so that's all that matters!"

Riveria winner
Max Homa

2021 Men's Majors

It was almost business-as-usual for the men's golf majors in 2021. The crowds were back, the Masters roars were back, and the British Open was back! But the results were anything but routine: a couple of unique champions kicked off an exciting majors season.

Masterful ▲

Omedetou, Hideki! That means "congratulations" to **Hideki Matsuyama**, the first Japanese golfer to win a men's major golf championship. The 29-year-old did it by winning the 2021 Masters tournament. Matsuyama made his move on the back nine on Saturday. He posted four birdies and an eagle during a seven-hole stretch. Matsuyama had a final-round 73 to win the tournament by one stroke over Masters rookie **Will Zalatoris**.

Old Guys Rule!

Before 50-year-old **Phil Mickelson** teed it up at the PGA Championship in May 2021, no player older than 48 had ever won one of golf's major titles. But after four days at the brutally tough Ocean Course in Kiawah Island, South Carolina, "Lefty" stood atop the leaderboard with a 6-under-par total of 282. He was two strokes clear of runners-up **Brooks Koepka** and **Louis Oosthuizen**.

Viva Golf!

Jon Rahm became the first golfer from Spain to win the U.S. Open with a one-stroke win over Oosthuizen at Torrey Pines. It was extra memorable for Rahm because it came on Father's Day and he got to hold his two-month-old son on the 18th green.

British Open

Young American star **Collin Morikawa** became the first player under 24 years old to win two majors in his first try. After winning the 2020 PGA Championship, the Californian flew across the pond to win the British Open in his first "go," as they say over there.

MEN'S MAJOR CHAMPIONS 2021	
MASTERS	**Hideki Matsuyama**
PGA CHAMPIONSHIP	**Phil Mickelson**
US OPEN	**Jon Rahm**
BRITISH OPEN	**Collin Morikawa**

2020 Women's Majors

The most noticeable difference in the 2020 women's major championship season was that the number of majors was reduced from five to four, when the COVID pandemic forced the cancellation of the Evian Championship.

Surprise Champ

In a change from other years, the Women's British Open kicked off the majors in 2020. **Sophia Popov** made it a memorable one with a two-shot victory at the historic Royal Troon Golf Club in Troon, South Ayrshire, Scotland. Popov was born in the United States and raised in Germany before playing college golf at USC. She entered the British Open as the 304th-ranked player in the world. She had never won an LPGA tournament!

Off the Backboard

South Korean golfer **Mirim Lee** used a little luck—and a little planning—to win her first major at the 2020 ANA Inspiration. Lee banked her second shot on the par-5 18th hole off a temporary wall behind the green. Then she chipped in for an eagle that got her into a three-way playoff. She won the playoff on the first extra hole.

Runaway Winner

One month after fellow South Korean Mirim Lee won her first major, **Sei Young Kim** did the same, breezing to a five-shot win at the Women's PGA Championship. Kim entered the tournament as the winningest player on the LPGA Tour without a major, but she left little doubt in this one. She shot a stunning 7-under-par 63 in a final round that included four birdies in a five-hole stretch of the back nine.

'Tis the Season

Eleven days before Christmas, **A Lim Kim** wrapped up a chilly comeback to win the U.S. Women's Open in Houston, Texas. The final round was postponed due to rain. When they finally played, it was so cold that Kim wore a parka between taking shots! She trailed by five strokes when the round began, but closed with three straight birdies. Her five-shot comeback tied for the best ever.

Sei Young Kim

2021 Women's Golf Notes

What a Walk-Off!

Just two months after men's golfer **Sergio Garcia** won a match with a rare feat (see page 161), Englishwoman **Bronte Law** ended her match the same way against **Austin Ernst**. It came during the second round of group play at the LPGA's Match Play event in Las Vegas. Law came to the 17th hole one shot ahead of Ernst. She needed to win one of the last two holes—or tie them both—to take the match. The end came quickly. Law drained her tee shot on the 154-yard par-3. American **Ally Ewing** ended up winning the event.

Sorenstam showed she's still got it!

Big Hitter

In June 2021, a 19-year-old won the US Women's Open in San Francisco (see page 165). Another teenager, 14-year-old **Chloe Kovelesky**, missed the cut. But Kovelesky wowed fellow pros and spectators both on the course and on the driving range with her booming tee shots. The youngest player in the tournament field, Kovelesky can regularly launch drives covering 280–290 yards. In 2020, the longest LPGA golfer only went 283 yards!

The GOAT

That's Greatest of All-Time, of course. In women's golf, there's little doubt we are talking about **Annika Sorenstam**. The 72-time winner on the LPGA Tour didn't have anything left to prove. But just to remind people of her greatness, Sorenstam teed it up at the LPGA stop in Orlando, Florida, in February 2021. At the age of 50, she faced players who were less than half her age, but she shot a second-round 71 to make the cut.

Tears of Joy

The University of Mississippi women's golf team won the 2021 NCAA championship. As head coach of the winning team, **Kory Henkes** was allowed to choose one player to get a shot at an LPGA event. Henkes chose **Julia Johnson**. But then Johnson said, "I would then in turn like to award the spot to **Kennedy Swann**," Johnson said. Swann was overcome with emotion at the selfless gift from her teammate.

Women's 2021 Majors

ANA Inspiration

Patty Tavatanakit of Thailand fired an opening-round 66 to take the lead at the season's first major in Rancho Mirage, California, and she never looked back en route to a two-stroke victory over former world No. 1 **Lydia Ko** of South Korea. It was the first LPGA victory of any kind for Tavatanakit, who turned pro in 2020 after playing at UCLA. After a short par putt on 18 to finish off a four-day total of 18 under par, Tavatanakit took the traditional winner's leap into Poppie's Pond next to the final green. What a great way to beat the 100-degree heat in the desert!

U.S. Women's Open

Yuka Saso became the first golfer from the Philippines to win a major. She also equaled **Inbee Park** as the youngest winner of the U.S. Women's Open. Like Saso in 2021, Inbee was 19 years, 11 months, and 17 days old when

Korda put an American back on top!

she won the tournament in '08. Trailing by three with three holes to go, Saso made a stunning comeback. She birdied 16 and 17. And though she just missed a birdie try at the 18th, her par got her into a playoff with **Nasa Hataoka** of Japan. On the third extra hole, Saso drained a 12-foot birdie putt to win.

Whoa, Nelly!

Twenty-two-year-old **Nelly Korda** from Bradenton, Florida, won the Women's PGA Championship at the Atlanta Athletic Club in June 2021. With the victory, she became the first American to win a women's major championship since 2018, and she rose to No. 1 in the world rankings.

WOMEN'S MAJOR CHAMPIONS 2021	
ANA INSPIRATION	**Patty Tavatanakit**
U.S. WOMEN'S OPEN	**Yuka Saso**
WOMEN'S PGA CHAMPIONSHIP	**Nelly Korda**
THE EVIAN CHAMPIONSHIP	**Minjee Lee**
WOMEN'S BRITISH OPEN	**Anna Nordqvist**

TENNIS

BIG WIN DOWN UNDER
Naomi Osaka continued her rise to the top of the tennis world with her second straight Australian Open win. She beat Jennifer Brady to win her fourth Grand Slam event. Osaka later took some time off before the Olympics for a mental-health break, for which she rightly got lots of praise. How did she do in the Olympics? Check out page 34!

2020 Grand Slams

Due to COVID, the 2020 Wimbledon event was canceled. But the US Open and the French Open went on, though without fans in the stands.

2020 US OPEN

At the US Open, Japan's **Naomi Osaka** lost the first set 6-1 to **Victoria Azarenka** of Belarus. "I thought, it would be very embarrassing to lose in under an hour," Osaka said. She regrouped and took each of the next two sets 6-3 to win the US Open for the second time in her career. It was her third Grand Slam victory in all.

On the men's side, the story wasn't so much who won—**Dominic Thiem**—but who didn't: none of the Big Three of **Novak Djokovic**, **Roger Federer**, and **Rafael Nadal**. Federer and Nadal didn't play in the tournament, and Djokovic was disqualified from a fourth-round match after whacking a line judge with a ball in a fit of anger. Thiem, a 27-year-old Austrian, won his first Grand Slam.

Świątek with her historic trophy.

2020 FRENCH OPEN

The women's final featured a pair of surprise athletes. American **Sofia Kenin** had never reached a quarterfinal on clay. **Iga Świątek** was ranked 54th in the world, the lowest-ranked French Open finalist since 1975. The Polish teenager had one more surprise: She won, beating Kenin in straight sets. She became the first tennis player from Poland to win a Grand Slam title.

The men's final included a pair of more familiar names: No. 1 Djokovic and No. 2 Nadal. Few players in history have been as good at one event as Nadal has been in France. He swooped over Djokovic to win the French Open for the 13th time, extending his record there. The Grand Slam win also gave him 20 for his career, tying Federer for the most ever.

2020 ATP Championships

The top four men in the world met in the two semifinals. In the final, **Daniil Medvedev** completed his amazing run from No. 4 to the championship. The Russian player became the first man since 1990 to beat the top three seeds at one finals event. Note: The 2020 WTA Finals for women were cancelled due to COVID restrictions.

2021 Grand Slams

The tennis world looked a lot more familiar in 2021. Grand Slam events returned to their usual spots on the calendar, fans (partially) returned to the stands, and Novak Djokovic returned to center stage.

Quick Work

Osaka needed fewer than 90 minutes to beat American **Jennifer Brady** in straight sets for her second Australian Open title. She became only the third player ever to win her fourth Grand Slam title in her fourth trip to a finals match.

Djokovic made it three Aussies in a row with his win over the emerging Russian star Medvedev.

French Firsts

In the final, neither player had ever won a Grand Slam. That changed, of course, when **Barbora Krejčíková** of the Czech Republic beat **Anastasia Pavlyuchenkova** of Russia in three sets.

On the men's side, Djokovic defeated **Stefanos Tsitsipas** of Greece. The Serbian star became the first man to win seven Grand Slam events after turning 30, and the first man in the Open Era (since 1968) to complete a double career Grand Slam—that is, winning each of the four major events at least twice.

Three-Quarter Slam

The amazing Djokovic took a major step toward history when he beat Italian **Matteo Berrettini** in four sets to win the men's singles title at the 2021 Wimbledon. It was Djokovic's 20th Grand Slam championship, pulling him even with Federer and Nadal for the most ever. It also was his third

Grand Slam title of the year. That sent him to the US Open in August/September with a chance to become only the second player in the Open Era to win all four men's Grand Slam championships in a calendar year. How did he do? It happened after we printed the book! Good luck, Novak!

Women's No. 1 **Ash Barty** of Australia kept it going en route to winning her first Wimbledon's singles title.

Djokovic put together a memorable 2021.

Tennis News 2020-21

Greek player Maria Sakkari on French clay.

From Bricks to Dust

Ever watch the French Open and wonder where all that red clay on the court comes from? Well, it comes from a factory in Oise, an area less than 60 miles (96.6 km) from Paris. A company there crushes a special kind of brick made in France. It grinds them so fine that it feels like sand. A layer of that clay is then spread over the courts at Roland-Garros over other layers of crushed limestone, clinker (coal residue), and crushed gravel. It takes 1.1 tons of red clay to build a single tennis court.

Rare Occurrence

Something strange happened to **Naomi Osaka** at the Miami Open in the spring of 2021: she lost. When Osaka fell to **Maria Sakkari** of Greece in straight sets in the quarterfinals, she dropped a match for the first time in 13 months. The upset defeat ended Osaka's string of 23 wins in a row—a streak that included victories in two Grand Slam finals—dating to February 2020.

Old Rafa, Meet the New Rafa

Rafael Nadal, who turned 35 in 2021, has been the king of Spanish tennis for more than a decade. But the 20-time Grand Slam singles champion may have met the future of the sport in his home country. **Carlos Alcaraz** played Nadal on his 18th birthday in the 2021 Madrid Open. Reporters called it the "Battle of Generations." Nadal won and proved he is still the king. But he said that Alcaraz "has enormous potential ahead of him. All he needs is some time."

Mother's Day

Here's something else that doesn't happen very often. Okay, it had never happened before. When **Victoria Azarenka** and **Serena Williams** met in the semifinals of the US Open in September 2020, it marked the first time that two moms squared off in the semifinals of a Grand Slam event. Azarenka, who gave birth to a son in December 2016, won the match over Williams, whose daughter was born the following year. It was Azarenka's first win over her American rival in 12 Grand Slam singles matches.

Hard-hitting Sofia Kenin is leading an American charge in women's tennis.

U-S-A! U-S-A!

The future looks bright for American women's tennis. Three players entered the summer of 2021 ranked among the top 15 in the world: No. 6 **Sofia Kenin**, No. 8 Serena Williams, and No. 15 **Jennifer Brady**. And although Williams was 39, several other stars 21 or younger appear poised to step up. **Coco Gauff**, who reached the fourth round at Wimbledon, was just 17 at the time and ranked No. 23 in the world. Twenty-one-year-old **Ann Li** was No. 72, and 19-year-old **Amanda Anisimova** was No. 81.

GRAND SLAM SINGLES TITLES

Novak Djokovic's incredible run of three titles to open the 2021 Grand Slam season (see page 169) gave him a men's record-tying 20 such championships in his career. **Serena Williams** (*right*) holds the women's record with 23 titles. Here are the women and men with the most Grand Slam singles titles in the Open Era* (since 1968):

WOMEN'S GRAND SLAMS		MEN'S GRAND SLAMS	
PLAYER	TITLES	PLAYER	TITLES
Serena WILLIAMS	23	Novak DJOKOVIC	20
Steffi GRAF	22	Roger FEDERER	20
Chris EVERT	18	Rafael NADAL	20
Martina NAVRATILOVA	18	Pete SAMPRAS	14
Margaret COURT	11	Björn BORG	11

*Does not include 2021 US Open.

OTHER SPORTS

SPEED ON THE WATER
Team New Zealand (right) trails Italy in this photo, but that is not how the America's Cup ended up. In a series of thrilling, high-speed races in Auckland, the hometown Kiwis kept the Cup after the nine-game series. The America's Cup started way back in 1851, making it one of the oldest sports events around.

Winter Sports

FIGURE SKATING

A year ahead of the 2022 Winter Olympics, American skater **Nathan Chen** showed that he'll be a big medal favorite. First, Chen won his fifth US national title. That is the most by a single skater since 1952! In the world championships, he won for the third time in a row. No American has done that since **Scott Hamilton** won his fourth title in 1984.

At the national championships, **Bradie Tennell** came in first, while **Karen Chen** earned the bronze. At the worlds, Karen Chen (no relation to Nathan) made a big leap, finishing fourth behind champion **Anna Shcherbakova** of Russia. American ice dancers **Madison Hubbell** and **Zachary Donohue** earned a silver at the world championships, too.

Nathan Chen

Slalom specialist Petra Vlhova won her first overall World Cup championship.

SKIING

With the retirement of champions skiers such as American superstar **Lindsey Vonn** and Austrian **Marcel Hirscher**, the World Cup races were wide open in 2021. World Cup racers pile up points week after week in events around Europe. Slovakia's **Petra Vlhova** was the women's champ, while also leading in parallel slalom points. France's **Alexis Pinturault** was the men's championship thanks to his giant slalom and parallel slalom titles.

At the 2021 World Championships, held on one weekend in Italy, **Mikaela Shiffrin** brought home a big haul of medals. The only American to medal, she won gold in the Super Combined, silver in giant slalom, and bronzes in slalom and Super-G.

Shiffrin shows off her Super Combined gold.

More Winter Sports

BOBSLED RACING

Germany's **Francesco Friedrich** became the first driver to win four straight World Championships in four-man bobsled when he won the 2021 event in his home nation. He also won the two-man competition.

The monobob event is for a single rider on a special sled. American **Kaillie Humphries** won the gold medal at the 2021 women's world championships. Kaillie also piloted the two-woman sled along with pusher **Lolo Jones** to another gold medal.

Humphries was the solo champ.

SPEED SKATING

Ireen Wüst helped the Netherlands win gold in the 3,000-meter pursuit event at the 2021 world championships. That gave her 31 all-time medals at the worlds, the most ever.

Nils van der Poel won gold in the 5,000-meter, the first ever for a skater from Sweden. Then he surprised fans with a world record in the difficult 10,000-meter race.

The World Short-Track Speedskating Championships were pretty quiet. Some countries could not send any racers, while others were very limited due to COVID. However, that didn't stop **Suzanne Schulting** of the Netherlands from dominating. She won all four gold medals in individual races from 500 to 1,500 meters. She won a fifth gold in the 3,000-meter relay.

Suzanne Schulting

Winter X Games

There were no fans at this annual ski and snowboard event, but the stars came out anyway. Every athlete who won a 2018 Olympic medal was part of the 2021 Winter X Games! American star **Jamie Anderson** led the way with two golds to give her eight all-time in the X Games. Her total medal count of 19 is one shy of **Mark McMorris**'s all-time record.

Chloe Kim became a world star with her gold in the 2018 Olympics, and she kept shining brightly in Aspen. She won snowboard superpipe in 2021, her fifth gold at the X Games. And she's only 20 years old!

With three medals, including gold in ski slopestyle, **Eileen Gu** won the most medals

Chloe Kim and Haruna Matsumoto: All smiles!

by any Chinese skier in X Games history. She was also the first woman to win three medals in one X Games as a rookie to the event.

2021 WINTER X GAMES CHAMPS

WOMEN'S SNOWBOARD SLOPESTYLE	**JAMIE ANDERSON**
WOMEN'S SKI BIG AIR	**MATHILDE GREMAUD**
SNOWBOARD KNUCKLE HUCK	**DUSTY HENRICKSEN**
WOMEN'S SKI SUPERPIPE	**NICO PORTEOUS**
WOMEN'S SKI SLOPESTYLE	**EILEEN GU**
MEN'S SKI BIG AIR	**ANDRI RAGETTLI**
WOMEN'S SNOWBOARD SUPERPIPE	**CHLOE KIM**
MEN'S SNOWBOARD SLOPESTYLE	**DUSTY HENRICKSEN**
MEN'S SKI SLOPESTYLE	**NICK GOEPPER**
WOMEN'S SNOWBOARD BIG AIR	**JAMIE ANDERSON**
MEN'S SNOWBOARD SUPERPIPE	**YUTO TOTSUKA**
MEN'S SNOWBOARD BIG AIR	**MARCUS KLEVELAND**
SKI KNUCKLE HUCK	**HENRIK HARLAUT**

Ferdinand Dahl in slopestyle.

Horse Racing

Authentic was a surprise 2020 winner.

2020 Belmont Stakes: The COVID crisis shuffled the order of the Triple Crown races. This race came first instead of last. **Tiz the Law**, born in New York, was the winner. He was the first Belmont champ from the race's home state since 1882!

2020 Kentucky Derby: This famous race was moved from May to September. Tiz the Law came in as one of the biggest favorites in recent history. But **Authentic** took a late lead from the outside and held off the favorite. It was the sixth victory for trainer **Bob Baffert**.

2020 Preakness: In October, Authentic nearly added another win to his total, but **Swiss Skydiver** held him off. She was only the second filly (that's a female horse!) to win this race since 1924!

2021 Kentucky Derby: Baffert trained another winner in **Medina Spirit**— or so it seemed. A post-race test found that the horse had an illegal drug in its system. Baffert was suspended, the horse probably disqualified, making **Mandaloun** the winner. The investigation continues.

2021 Preakness: Medina Spirit was allowed to run this race, but **Rombauer** ended up running away with the trophy after a powerful late run. That gave jockey **Flavian Prat** a win in his first Preakness Stakes.

2021 Belmont Stakes:
Essential Quality beat **Hot Rod Charlie** in this race in New York.

Known as AC75s, America's Cup boats use parts called "foils" to soar through the water.

America's Cup

The America's Cup sailing race was first held way back in 1851. Since then, all kinds of ships have been used, mostly giant yachts. In recent years, though, boat designers have used high-tech sails, flying wings, and tons of computer modeling. The results are the amazing craft shown in this picture. At top speed, they can move as fast as a car on the freeway!

In 2021, Team New Zealand defended its Cup championship against a boat from Italy. The two teams battled in the waters of Auckland Harbor in a series of races. The hometown Kiwis broke open a tight contest with three straight race wins. The last was No. 7, enough to clinch the Cup.

Team New Zealand had the right man as the skipper. **Peter Burling** was the captain in the last Cup, and he has also won nine world championships. Oh, and he also has an Olympic gold medal in sailing!

Race Results
RACE/WINNER

1 Team New Zealand
2 Luna Rossa Prada Pirelli
3 Luna Rossa Prada Pirelli
4 Team New Zealand
5 Luna Rossa Prada Pirelli
6 Team New Zealand
7 Team New Zealand
8 Team New Zealand
9 Team New Zealand

Tour de France

2020

The long and difficult Tour de France cycling races test riders on flat road, high mountains, and in painful time trials. In 2020's race, held in September, **Primož Roglič** did the best of all until the next-to-last day. He led fellow Slovenian rider **Tadej Pogačar** by almost a minute as the final time trial began. When it was over, it was Pogačar who led by a minute. It was a shocking turnaround. "I went full gas from the bottom to the top," said a surprised Pogačar. After a final leg of the race around Paris, Pogačar became the second-youngest winner ever at 21 years old.

Pogačar was No. 1 . . . twice!

Kuss powered to a big win.

2021

Two in a row! Pogačar became the youngest rider ever with two Tour de France titles. Unlike in 2020, he moved to the overall lead quickly. The rider from Slovenia was in first place after the eighth of the race's 21 stages. He powered over difficult climbing stages like they were quiet country lanes. Along with the overall trophy, he earned the title "King of the Mountains."

English rider **Mark Cavendish** tied an all-time record with his 34th career stage victory. And American **Sepp Kuss** won Stage 15. It was the first such win by a US rider since 2011.

Track and Field

The Summer Olympics (page 18) were the site for most of the track and field highlights of the past year. But some other athletes made news by running and jumping.

Up, Up, and Away!

French pole vaulter **Armand Duplantis** set a new world record—twice! In February 2020, he soared 20 feet, 2¾ inches (6.17 m). A week later, he went even higher, adding an inch to his record (6.18 m). Only 19, Duplantis has his eye on even bigger records. "I can't see any reason why I can't jump higher than I've already jumped right now, for sure."

Run, Run, Run!

The long-distance races call for endurance and courage. These amazing athletes can keep their speed up lap after lap. In June 2020, **Joshua Cheptegei** of Uganda broke the world record in the 5,000-meter run. He did it in 12 minutes, 35.36 seconds. Two months later, he put himself atop the record book in the 10,000 meters. He covered that distance (more than six miles!) in 26 minutes, 11 seconds. Ethiopia's **Letesenbet Gidey** set the women's mark for the 10,000 at 14 minutes, 6.62 seconds.

Duplantis knew he had the new record!

Oops

American **Noah Lyles** appeared to set a world record in the 200-meter race at a meet in Switzerland. He sped around the track in 18.9 seconds, beating **Usain Bolt**'s mark of 19.19. However, it turned out that event organizers had Lyles begin on the wrong starting line. In the 200, racers don't start at the same place, but slightly ahead of each other to make up for the curve of the track. So Lyles did what he was told—and ran only 185 meters, not 200! So no record, but a lesson for meet organizers, who apologized for their error.

Lacrosse

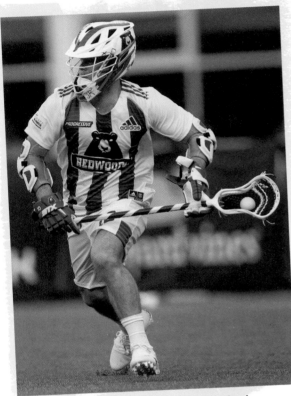

Action from a 2021 PLL contest.

This is one of the fastest-growing sports in America. More high schools are adding the sport, and clubs are popping up all over. Of course, COVID caused a big "time-out" in 2020, but there was important lacrosse news. Major League Lacrosse was the top pro league in the US. It began in 2001. Then the Premier Lacrosse League began in 2019 and was quickly getting many top players to sign up. There were not quite enough players and fans for both leagues, so they decided to team up! Starting in late 2021, the expanded eight-team PLL played the first season after the team-up. The season ended after we had to print, so go online and find out who the champion was!

Lacrosse PS: The indoor National Lacrosse League didn't restart until December 2021.

2021 PLL CHAMP

_____

THANKS, IRISH! Thousands of years ago, Native Americans were the first to play lacrosse. Today, nations including the Iroquois still field top teams. However, at first, the Iroquois were not allowed into the 2022 Lacrosse World Games. The lacrosse community complained long and hard. Finally, the sport's world leaders said okay, the Iroquois could play. However, all the teams in the playoffs were all set. So Ireland's team said it would stay home in order to let the Iroquois play. Great sportsmanship! On Twitter, the Iroquois Nationals team wrote, "You have gone above and beyond not only for us, but for what you believe is right. Your actions show the true power of sport, and the spirit of lacrosse."

COLLEGE BASEBALL & SOFTBALL

OU star Giselle Juarez

Congrats to Oklahoma for winning the 2021 Women's College World Series in softball. The power-hitting Sooners had to overcome a shocking early-round loss to James Madison. They battled back to beat Florida State in the finals to earn their fifth national championship.

In baseball, Mississippi State won the College World Series in Omaha, the school's first-ever national title in any sport. They upset Vanderbilt in three games. The clinching game was a pitching gem. Mississippi State allowed the Commodores only one hit. Then it was time for the big dogpile on the infield!

Surfing

How high was the awesome world-record wave that **Maya Gabeira** rode? Find a building near you that is seven stories tall. Or imagine three school buses standing end-on-end. Those are about the same height as the 73.5-foot wall the Brazilian star rode. Gabeira was surfing in the Nazare Challenge, off the coast of Portugal. At the right time of year, that spot has some of the highest waves in the world. Gabeira dropped in and zoomed down the face of the massive wall of water. Wow!

USC dug out
another beach
volleyball title.

NCAA Champions 2020–21

Most college sports returned in the 2020–21 school year. Here's a list of the Division 1 winners. This list doesn't include sports covered elsewhere in the book, such as baseball/softball, basketball, and football. Also, some sports are only played by men or women in the NCAA.

SPORTS	WOMEN	MEN
BEACH VOLLEYBALL	USC	
BOWLING	NEBRASKA	
CROSS-COUNTRY	BYU	NORTHERN ARIZONA
FIELD HOCKEY	NORTH CAROLINA	
GOLF	MISSISSIPPI	PEPPERDINE
GYMNASTICS	MICHIGAN	STANFORD
ICE HOCKEY	WISCONSIN	MASSACHUSETTS
INDOOR TRACK	ARKANSAS	OREGON
LACROSSE	BOSTON COLLEGE	VIRGINIA
OUTDOOR TRACK	USC	LSU
SOCCER	SANTA CLARA	MARSHALL
SWIMMING/DIVING	VIRGINIA	TEXAS
TENNIS	TEXAS	FLORIDA
VOLLEYBALL	KENTUCKY	HAWAII
WATER POLO	USC	UCLA
WRESTLING		IOWA

Marshall's men ran to the title.

Soccer

Men's college soccer saw a first-time champ in 2021. **Jamil Roberts** scored in overtime to give Marshall a win over powerhouse Indiana 1-0. The women's team was a repeat champ. Santa Clara won in 2001, and then again in 2021 thanks to a penalty-kick shootout victory over Florida State.

Golf

With a 4-1 win over Oklahoma State, Mississippi's women's team won their school's first-ever title in this sport. It was also the first national title by any Ole Miss team since 1962! The men's champion was Pepperdine, which had also won back in 1997. Their championship win over Oklahoma was a bit closer, 3-2.

Wrestling

Iowa has dominated men's wrestling. The Hawkeyes had won 23 titles since their first one back in 1975. But they had not been on top since 2010. That changed in 2021, as they finished first ahead of Penn State and Oklahoma State at the championship meet. **Spencer Lee** led the way by earning his third title in the 125-pound class.

Ice Hockey

One thing was sure before the start of the men's hockey final: There would be a first-time champ. Neither Massachusetts nor St. Cloud State (from Minnesota) had ever won a national title, though both schools had come close. **Aaron Bohlinger** of Massachusetts picked a good time to score his first college goal. His score was the start of a 5-0 rout for UMass. Goalie **Filip Lindberg** from Finland was the first goalie born outside North America to win the title. The Wisconsin women won their sixth title, thanks to an overtime goal by **Daryl Watts** that she bounced in off the Northeastern goalie.

Beach Volleyball

Two teams from California had to go all the way to Alabama to win the beach volleyball title. USC beat UCLA 3-1 in the final to earn its fourth championship in the sandy sport.

Iowa wrestler Jayden Eierman

CHAMPIONS!

NFL

GAME	SEASON	RESULT
LV	2021	**Tampa Bay** 31, **Kansas City** 9
LIV	2020	**Kansas City** 31, **San Francisco** 20
LIII	2019	**New England** 13, **Los Angeles** 3
LII	2018	**Philadelphia** 41, **New England** 33
LI	2017	**New England** 34, **Atlanta** 28
50	2016	**Denver** 24, **Carolina** 10
XLIX	2015	**New England** 28, **Seattle** 24
XLVIII	2014	**Seattle** 43, **Denver** 8
XLVII	2013	**Baltimore** 34, **San Francisco** 31
XLVI	2012	**New York** 21, **New England** 17
XLV	2011	**Green** Bay 31, **Pittsburgh** 25

Rodgers won his second MVP in 2020.

NFL MOST VALUABLE PLAYER

2020	**Aaron RODGERS**, Green Bay
2019	**Lamar JACKSON**, Baltimore
2018	**Patrick MAHOMES**, Kansas City
2017	**Tom BRADY**, New England
2016	**Matt RYAN**, Atlanta
2015	**Cam NEWTON**, Carolina
2014	**Aaron RODGERS**, Green Bay
2013	**Peyton MANNING**, Denver
2012	**Adrian PETERSON**, Minnesota
2011	**Aaron RODGERS**, Green Bay

COLLEGE FOOTBALL

2020 **ALABAMA**	2014 **OHIO STATE**
2019 **LSU**	2013 **FLORIDA ST.**
2018 **CLEMSON**	2012 **ALABAMA**
2017 **ALABAMA**	2011 **ALABAMA**
2016 **CLEMSON**	2010 **AUBURN**
2015 **ALABAMA**	

Here's a handy guide to recent winners and champions of most of the major sports. They've all been celebrated in past editions of the YEAR IN SPORTS. But here they are all together again!

MLB

2020 Los Angeles **DODGERS** 4, Tampa Bay **RAYS** 2
2019 Washington **NATIONALS** 4, Houston **ASTROS** 3
2018 Boston **RED SOX** 4, Los Angeles **DODGERS** 1
2017 Houston **ASTROS** 4, Los Angeles **DODGERS** 3
2016 Chicago **CUBS** 4, Cleveland **INDIANS** 3
2015 Kansas City **ROYALS** 4, New York **METS** 1
2014 San Francisco **GIANTS** 4, Kansas City **ROYALS** 3
2013 Boston **RED SOX** 4, St. Louis **CARDINALS** 2
2012 San Francisco **GIANTS** 4, Detroit **TIGERS** 0
2011 St. Louis **CARDINALS** 4, Texas **RANGERS** 3
2010 San Francisco **GIANTS** 4, Texas **RANGERS** 1

MLB MOST VALUABLE PLAYER

	AL	NL
2020	JOSÉ **ABREU**	FREDDIE FREEMAN
2019	MIKE **TROUT**	CODY **BELLINGER**
2018	MOOKIE **BETTS**	CHRISTIAN **YELICH**
2017	JOSÉ **ALTUVE**	GIANCARLO **STANTON**
2016	MIKE **TROUT**	KRIS **BRYANT**
2015	JOSH **DONALDSON**	BRYCE **HARPER**
2014	MIKE **TROUT**	CLAYTON **KERSHAW**
2013	MIGUEL **CABRERA**	ANDREW **MCCUTCHEN**
2012	MIGUEL **CABRERA**	BUSTER **POSEY**
2011	JUSTIN **VERLANDER**	RYAN **BRAUN**

COLLEGE BASKETBALL

YEAR	MEN'S	WOMEN'S
2021	Baylor	Stanford
2020	Not played	Not played
2019	Virginia	Baylor
2018	Villanova	Notre Dame
2017	N. Carolina	S. Carolina
2016	Villanova	Connecticut
2015	Duke	Connecticut
2014	Connecticut	Connecticut
2013	Louisville	Connecticut
2012	Kentucky	Baylor
2011	Connecticut	Texas A&M
2010	Duke	Connecticut

NHL

2021 **Lightning 4**, Canadiens 1
2020 **Lightning 4**, Stars 2
2019 **Blues 4**, Bruins 3
2018 **Capitals 4**, Golden Knights 1
2017 **Penguins 4**, Predators 2
2016 **Penguins 4**, Sharks 2
2015 **Blackhawks 4**, Lightning 2
2014 **Kings 4**, Rangers 1
2013 **Blackhawks 4**, Bruins 2
2012 **Kings 4**, Devils 2
2011 **Bruins 4**, Canucks 3

Four WNBA titles for Sue Bird and Seattle.

NBA

2021 **Milwaukee Bucks**
2020 **Los Angeles Lakers**
2019 **Toronto Raptors**
2018 **Golden State Warriors**
2017 **Golden State Warriors**
2016 **Cleveland Cavaliers**
2015 **Golden State Warriors**
2014 **San Antonio Spurs**
2013 **Miami Heat**
2012 **Miami Heat**
2011 **Dallas Mavericks**

WNBA

2021 _____
2020 **Seattle Storm**
2019 **Washington Mystics**
2018 **Seattle Storm**
2017 **Minnesota Lynx**
2016 **Los Angeles Sparks**
2015 **Minnesota Lynx**
2014 **Phoenix Mercury**
2013 **Minnesota Lynx**
2012 **Indiana Fever**
2011 **Minnesota Lynx**

MLS

2020	**Columbus Crew**
2019	**Seattle Sounders**
2018	**Atlanta United FC**
2017	**Toronto FC**
2016	**Seattle Sounders**
2015	**Portland Timbers**
2014	**Los Angeles Galaxy**
2013	**Sporting Kansas City**

NWSL

2020	**Canceled**
2019	**North Carolina Courage**
2018	**North Carolina Courage**
2017	**Portland Thorns FC**
2016	**Western New York Flash**
2015	**FC Kansas City**
2014	**FC Kansas City**
2013	**Portland Thorns FC**

FIFA WORLD PLAYER OF THE YEAR*

Year	Men	Women
2020	Robert **Lewandowski**	Lucy **Bronze**
2019	Lionel **Messi**	Megan **Rapinoe**#
2018	Luka **Modrić**	**Marta**
2017	Cristiano **Ronaldo**	Lieke **Martens**
2016	Cristiano **Ronaldo**	Carli **Lloyd**#
2015	Lionel **Messi**	Carli **Lloyd**#
2014	Cristiano **Ronaldo**	Nadine **Keßler**
2013	Cristiano **Ronaldo**	Nadine **Angerer**
2012	Lionel **Messi**	Abby **Wambach**#
2011	Lionel **Messi**	Homare **Sawa**

* was known as the FIFA Ballon d'Or [Golden Ball] from 2010-15.   # from the United States

PGA Player of the Year

2020	Dustin **Johnson**
2019	Brooks **Koepka**
2018	Brooks **Koepka**
2017	Justin **Thomas**
2016	Dustin **Johnson**
2015	Jordan **Spieth**
2014	Rory **McIlroy**
2013	Tiger **Woods**
2012	Rory **McIlroy**
2011	Luke **Donald**
2010	Jim **Furyk**

LPGA Player of the Year

2020	Sei Young **Kim**
2019	Jin Young **Ko**
2018	Ariya **Jutanugarn**
2017	Sung Hyun **Park** and So Yeon **Ryu**
2016	Ariya **Jutanugarn**
2015	Lydia **Ko**
2014	Stacy **Lewis**
2013	Inbee **Park**
2012	Stacy **Lewis**
2011	Yani **Tseng**
2010	Yani **Tseng**

ATP Player of the Year

2020	Novak **DJOKOVIC**
2019	Rafael **NADAL**
2018	Novak **DJOKOVIC**
2017	Rafael **NADAL**
2016	Andy **MURRAY**
2015	Novak **DJOKOVIC**
2014	Novak **DJOKOVIC**
2013	Rafael **NADAL**
2012	Novak **DJOKOVIC**
2011	Novak **DJOKOVIC**
2010	Rafael **NADAL**

WTA Player of the Year

2020	Ash **BARTY**
2019	Ash **BARTY**
2018	Simona **HALEP**
2017	Simona **HALEP**
2016	Angelique **KERBER**
2015	Serena **WILLIAMS**
2014	Serena **WILLIAMS**
2013	Serena **WILLIAMS**
2012	Victoria **AZARENKA**
2011	Caroline **WOZNIACKI**
2010	Caroline **WOZNIACKI**

NASCAR

2020	CHASE **ELLIOT**
2019	KYLE **BUSCH**
2018	JOEY **LOGANO**
2017	MARTIN **TRUEX JR.**
2016	JIMMIE **JOHNSON**
2015	KYLE **BUSCH**
2014	KEVIN **HARVICK**
2013	JIMMIE **JOHNSON**
2012	BRAD **KESELOWSKI**
2011	TONY **STEWART**

INDYCAR

2020	SCOTT **DIXON**
2019	JOSEF **NEWGARDEN**
2018	SCOTT **DIXON**
2017	JOSEF **NEWGARDEN**
2016	SIMON **PAGENAUD**
2015	SCOTT **DIXON**
2014	WILL **POWER**
2013	SCOTT **DIXON**
2012	RYAN **HUNTER-REAY**
2011	DARIO **FRANCHITTI**

FORMULA 1

2020	LEWIS **HAMILTON**
2019	LEWIS **HAMILTON**
2018	LEWIS **HAMILTON**
2017	LEWIS **HAMILTON**
2016	NICO **ROSBERG**
2015	LEWIS **HAMILTON**
2014	LEWIS **HAMILTON**
2013	SEBASTIAN **VETTEL**
2012	SEBASTIAN **VETTEL**
2011	SEBASTIAN **VETTEL**

DAYTONA 500 CHAMPIONS

2021	**Michael MCDOWELL**
2020	**Denny HAMLIN**
2019	**Denny HAMLIN**
2018	**Austin DILLON**
2017	**Kurt BUSCH**
2016	**Denny HAMLIN**
2015	**Joey LOGANO**
2014	**Dale EARNHARDT JR.**
2013	**Jimmie JOHNSON**
2012	**Matt KENSETH**

INDY 500 CHAMPIONS

2021	**Hélio CASTRONEVES**
2020	**Takuma SATO**
2019	**Simon PAGENAUD**
2018	**Will POWER**
2017	**Takuma SATO**
2016	**Alexander ROSSI**
2015	**Juan Pablo MONTOYA**
2014	**Ryan HUNTER-REAY**
2013	**Tony KANAAN**
2012	**Dario FRANCHITTI**

Castroneves and the traditional milk!

Produced by Shoreline Publishing Group LLC

Santa Barbara, California
www.shorelinepublishing.com
President/Editorial Director: James Buckley, Jr.
Designed by Tom Carling, www.carlingdesign.com

The text for *Scholastic Year in Sports 2022* was written by

James Buckley, Jr.

Editorial assistance, including Golf, Tennis, and NHL: **Jim Gigliotti**, **Beth Adelman**, and **Craig Zeichner**
Fact-checking: **Matt Marini**

Thanks to team captain Tiffany Colón, the photo squad of Emily Teresa and Marybeth Kavanagh, production pit crew chief Jael Fogle, and the superstars at Scholastic for all their championship work! Photo research was done by the author. The author would also like to dedicate this 13th edition of the *Scholastic Year in Sports* to the late Dick Robinson, longtime president and CEO of Scholastic. He was a lifelong leader in making sure books like this one were made to educate and entertain young readers. He will be missed.

• •

Photography Credits

Photos ©: cover top left: REUTERS/Alamy Stock Photo; cover top right: Tom Pennington/Getty Images; cover center: Xinhua/Alamy Stock Photo; cover center left: ZUMA Press/Alamy Stock Photo; cover center right: Peter Joneleit/Icon Sportswire/AP Images; cover bottom left: Mark Pain/Alamy Stock Photo; cover bottom center: UPI/Alamy Stock Photo; cover bottom right: Cal Sport Media/Alamy Stock Photo; cover background: Shutterstock.com; back cover top left: Leonard Zhukovsky/Shutterstock; back cover top right: Carmen Mandato/Getty Images; back cover bottom: Alika Jenner/Getty Images; 4: Justin Casterline/Getty Images; 5: Ethan Miller/Getty Images; 8: AP Photo/Bruna Prado; 9: Rudy Carezzevoli, Pool/AP Images; 10: Li Yibo/Xinhua/Getty Images; 11: Gregory Shamus/Getty Images; 12: Helen H. Richardson/MediaNews Group/The Denver Post/Getty Images; 13: AP Photo/Sue Ogrocki; 14: Matthew Emmons-USA TODAY Sports; 15: FRANCOIS-XAVIER MARIT/AFP/Getty Images; 16: Jamie Squire/Getty Images; 17: AP Photo/Kathy Willens; 18-19: JEWEL SAMAD/AFP/Getty Images; 20: Wally Skalij /Los Angeles Times/Getty Images; 21: Stephen Gosling/NBAE/Getty Images; 22 left: The Asahi Shimbun/Getty Images; 22 right: Kyodo News/Getty Images; 23 top: Laurence Griffiths/Getty Images; 23 bottom: The Asahi Shimbun/Getty Images; 24: Baptiste Fernandez/Icon Sport/Getty Images; 25: Simon Bruty/Sports Illustrated/Getty Images; 26: Fred Lee/Getty Images; 27 top: Wang Lili/Xinhua/Getty Images; 27 bottom: David Ramos/Getty Images; 28: Stanislav Krasilnikov/TASS/Getty Images; 29 top: Rick Madonik/Toronto Star/Getty Images; 29 bottom: Lu Yang/Xinhua/Getty Images; 30: Brian Cassella/Chicago Tribune/Tribune News Service/Getty Images; 31 top: The Asahi Shimbun/Getty Images; 31 bottom: The Asahi Shimbun/Getty Images; 32: Pim Waslander/BSR Agency/Getty Images; 33 top: Adam Davy/PA Images/Getty Images; 33 bottom: Li He/Xinhua/Getty Images; 34: Steph Chambers/Getty Images; 35 top: An Lingjun/CHINASPORTS/VCG/ Getty Images; 35 bottom: LUIS ACOSTA/AFP/Getty Images; 36-37: Kevin M. Cox/The Galveston County Daily News/AP Images; 38: Tim Heitman-USA TODAY Sports; 39: AP Photo/Chris O'Meara; 40: Nick Wosika/Icon Sportswire/AP Images; 41: AP Photo/Ted S. Warren; 42: Dale Zanine-USA TODAY Sports; 43: Orlando Ramirez-USA TODAY Sports; 44: Kyodo/AP Images; 45: Tim Heitman-USA TODAY Sports; 46: Jerome Miron-USA TODAY Sports; 47: Jay Biggerstaff-USA TODAY Sports; 48: John Cordes/Icon Sportswire/AP Images; 49: AP Photo/Ted S. Warren; 50-51: Mark J. Rebilas-USA TODAY Sports; 52 left: Ken Blaze-USA TODAY Sports; 52 right: Joe Robbins/AP Images; 53: Gary A. Vasquez-USA TODAY Sports; 54: AP Photo/Elaine Thompson; 55: Stephen R. Sylvanie-USA TODAY Sports; 56: Denny Medley-USA TODAY Sports; 57: Cooper Neill/AP Images; 58: Patrick Breen/The Republic via Imagn Content Services, LLC; 59: Ron Chenoy-USA TODAY Sports; 60: AP Photo/Tyler Kaufman; 61: Carlos Goldman/Miami Dolphins/AP Images; 62 left: Perry Knotts/AP Images; 62 right: Paul Spinelli/AP Images; 63: AP Photo/Stephen Brashear; 64: JAMIE GERMANO/ROCHESTER DEMOCRAT AND CHRONICLE via Imagn Content Services, LLC; 65: Denny Medley-USA TODAY Sports; 66 top: Matthew Emmons-USA TODAY Sports; 66 bottom: Mark J. Rebilas-USA TODAY Sports; 67: AP Photo/Mark Humphrey; 68: Rich Barnes-USA TODAY Sports; 69 top: Bill Streicher-USA TODAY Sports; 69 bottom: AP Photo/Elaine Thompson; 70-71: Kim Klement-USA TODAY Sports; 72 left: AP Photo/Mark Humphrey; 72 right: Jay Biggerstaff-USA TODAY Sports; 73: Handout Photo-USA TODAY Sports; 74: Jerome Miron-USA TODAY Sports; 75: Marc Lebryk-USA TODAY Sports; 76: Christopher Hanewinckel-USA TODAY Sports; 77: Gregory Fisher/Icon Sportswire/AP Images; 78: Keith Birmingham/The Orange County Register/AP Images; 79: AP Photo/Aaron Doster; 80: Chuck Cook-USA TODAY Sports; 81: Kim Klement-USA TODAY Sports; 82-83: Mark J. Rebilas-Pool/Getty Images; 84 left: Jim Poorten/NBAE via Getty Images; 84 right: AP Photo/Nam Y. Huh; 85: Brad Penner-USA TODAY Sports; 86: Kim Klement-USA TODAY Sports; 87: Kevin C. Cox/Pool Photo/AP Images; 88: Ashley Landis/Pool Photo-USA TODAY Sports; 89: Kim Klement-USA TODAY Sports; 90: Kim Klement-USA TODAY Sports; 91: AP Photo/Mark J. Terrill; 92: Geoff Burke-USA TODAY Sports; 93: Brett Davis-USA TODAY Sports; 94 left: AP Photo/Chris Szagola; 94 right: Steve Dykes-USA TODAY Sports; 95: Tommy Gilligan-USA TODAY Sports; 96: AP Photo/Brynn Anderson; 97: Jonathan Daniel/Getty Images; 98: Julio Aguilar/Getty Images; 99: Stephen Gosling/NBAE/Getty Images; 100: Julio Aguilar/Getty Images; 101: Ned Dishman/NBAE/Getty Images; 102-103: Tim Nwachukwu/Getty Images; 104 top: Kirby Lee-USA TODAY Sports; 104 bottom: Kirby Lee-USA TODAY Sports; 105: Mary Langenfeld-USA TODAY Sports; 106: Denny Medley-USA TODAY Sports; 107: AP Photo/Sean Rayford; 108: Joshua Bickel-USA TODAY Sports; 109: Marc Lebryk-USA TODAY Sports; 110: Trevor Brown Jr/NCAA Photos/Getty Images; 111: Robert Deutsch-USA TODAY Sports; 112: AP Photo/Eric Gay; 113: Troy Taormina-USA TODAY Sports; 114: Perry Nelson-USA TODAY Sports; 115: Kim Klement-USA TODAY Sports; 116: Jason Franson/The Canadian Press/AP Images; 117: Timothy T. Ludwig-USA TODAY Sports; 118: Jason Franson/The Canadian Press/AP Images; 119: Dan Hamilton-USA TODAY Sports; 120: Perry Nelson-USA TODAY Sports; 122: Ryan Remiorz/The Canadian Press/AP Images; 123: Douglas DeFelice-USA TODAY Sports; 124: Christopher Hanewinckel-USA TODAY Sports; 125: AP Photo/Gerry Broome; 126-127: Fran Santiago - UEFA/UEFA/Getty Images; 128: Andrew Bershaw/Icon Sportswire/Getty Images; 129: Andrew Bershaw/Icon Sportswire via Getty Images; 130: Andy Mead/ISI Photos/Getty Images; 131: Jeffrey Swinger-USA TODAY Sports; 132: Matthias Hangst/Getty Images; 133 top: David Lidstrom/Getty Images; 133 bottom: Darren Walsh/Chelsea FC via Getty Images; 134: Paul Ellis, Pool/AP Images; 135: Michael Regan/Getty Images; 136: AP Photo/Bruna Prado; 137 left: WILTON JUNIOR/ESTADAO CONTEUDO/Agencia Estado/AP Images; 137 right: AP Photo/Bruna Prado; 138: Jean-Christophe Bott/Keystone/AP Images; 139 top: ddp images/Sipa USA/AP Images; 139 bottom: Marvin Guengoerr/GES/Pool/ddp images/Sipa USA/AP Images; 140: Robin Alam/Icon Sportswire/AP Images; 141: Helen H. Richardson/MediaNews Group/The Denver Post/Getty Images; 142-143: David Rosenblum/Icon Sportswire/Getty Images; 143 inset: David Tucker/News Journal via Imagn Content Services, LLC; 144 top: Darron Cummings/Pool Photo via USA TODAY Network; 144 bottom: AP Photo/Jason Minto; 145: Mark J. Rebilas-USA TODAY Sports; 146: AP Photo/NKP, Russell LaBounty; 147: AP Photo/Ralph Freso; 148 top: AP Photo/Ralph Freso; 149: Randy Sartin-USA TODAY Sports; 150-151: TOLGA BOZOGLU/POOL/AFP/Getty Images; 152 top: Bryn Lennon/Getty Images; 152 bottom: Bryn Lennon/Getty Images; 153: ANDREW BOYERS/POOL/AFP/Getty Images; 154 bottom: Reinhold Matay-USA TODAY Sports; 154 top: Reinhold Matay-USA TODAY Sports; 155: Mark J. Rebilas-USA TODAY Sports; 156: Mark J. Rebilas-USA TODAY Sports; 156 inset: Mark J. Rebilas-USA TODAY Sports; 157 top: Thurman James/CSM/ZUMA Wire/AP Images; 157 bottom: Garth Milan/Red Bull Content Pool/AP Images; 158-159: David Yeazell-USA TODAY Sports; 160: AP Photo/John Minchillo; 161: AP Photo/Ryan Kang; 162: Rob Schumacher-USA TODAY Sports; 163: AP Photo/Chris Szagola; 164: AP Photo/John Raoux; 165: AP Photo/John Bazemore; 166-167: Jason Heidrich/Icon Sportswire/Getty Images; 168: AP Photo/Christophe Ena; 169: Peter van den Berg-USA TODAY Sports; 170: AP Photo/Thibault Camus; 171 top: AP Photo/Andy Brownbill; 171 bottom: Press Association/AP Images; 172-173: Phil Walter/Getty Images; 174: The Yomiuri Shimbun/AP Images; 175 top: Alexis Boichard/Agence Zoom/Getty Images; 175 bottom: ANDREAS SOLARO/AFP/Getty Images; 176 top: Martin Rose/Getty Images; 176 bottom: Andre Weening/BSR Agency/Getty Images; 177 top: Kelsey Brunner/The Aspen Times/AP Images; 177 bottom: Kelsey Brunner/The Aspen Times/AP Images; 178: Michael Clevenger/Courier Journal via Imagn Content Services, LLC; 179: GILLES MARTIN-RAGET/AFP/Getty Images; 180 left: AP Photo/Daniel Cole; 180 right: Tim de Waele/Getty Images; 181: ANDREAS SOLARO/AFP/Getty Images; 182: AP Photo/Steve Luciano; 183 top: Rob Ferguson-USA TODAY Sports; 183 bottom: Laurent Masurel/WSL/Getty Images; 184: C. Morgan Engel/NCAA Photos/Getty Images; 185 top: AP Photo/Karl B DeBlaker; 185 bottom: AP Photo/Jeff Roberson; 186: Jeff Hanisch-USA TODAY Sports; 188: AP Photo/Phelan M. Ebenhack; 191: Mark J. Rebilas-USA TODAY Sports.